THE AMERICAN IMAGE OF RUSSIA · 1775–1917

THE AMERICAN IMAGE

WITH 37 LINE DRAWINGS

A STEPPE VILLAGE

OF RUSSIA · 1775-1917

Edited with an Introduction and Comments by

Eugene Anschel

FREDERICK UNGAR PUBLISHING CO. · NEW YORK

ACKNOWLEDGMENTS

I am indebted to Professor Marc Raeff, of Columbia University, and to Professor Harry W. Nerhood, of Whittier College, for their interest in this project and various helpful suggestions.

Grateful acknowledgment for permission to reprint is made to the following: The Massachusetts Historical Society, for excerpts from John Quincy Adams, "Essay on Russia," from The Adams Papers; The University of Wisconsin Press, for excerpts from Stephen D. Watrous, ed., *John Ledyard's Journey through Russia and Siberia, 1787–1788*, © 1966 by the Regents of the University of Wisconsin; and The Historical Society of Delaware, for William David Lewis, "Letter to Edward Coles," printed in *Delaware History*.

ILLUSTRATION SOURCES

The line drawings appearing on the pages listed below have been taken from the following sources:

Pages 80, 86, 148: James Monroe Buckley, *The Midnight Sun, the Tsar and the Nihilist* (Boston, 1886).

Pages 42, 43 bottom, 44, 78 top: William Elroy Curtis, *Russia: The Land of the Nihilist* (Chicago, 1888).

Page 147 top: S. T. Evans, "Domestic Life in Russia," *Potter's American Monthly* (Philadelphia) 9 (July, 1877).

Pages 79 bottom, 101, 182 bottom: *Harper's New Monthly Magazine* (New York) 11 (September, 1855).

Pages, Frontis., 59, 60, 100 bottom, 162, 163, 234: George Kennan, *Siberia and the Exile System* (New York, 1891).

Pages 41, 43 top, 58, 79 top, 85, 100 top, 122, 136 bottom, 153, 164, 181, 182 top, 183, 209: Thomas W. Knox, *The Boy Travellers in the Russian Empire* (New York, 1886).

Pages 136 top, 147 bottom: Edna Dean Proctor, *A Russian Journey* (Boston, 1890).

Page 78 bottom: John L. Stoddard, *Red-Letter Days Abroad* (Boston, 1884).

Contents

List of Illustrations

Introduction

TOWARD THE END of 1775, Thomas Paine took stock of the world that would face the new nation. Russia, he reflected, was of scant importance to America. "The vast empire of Russia," he wrote in his *Common Sense*, "is almost shut out from the sea; wherefore her boundless forests, her tar, iron and cordage are only articles of commerce [for others]."[1] Not being a seafaring nation nor possessing maritime power, Russia appeared to play a small role in international affairs. Therefore her existence and resources, her enmity or friendship could mean little to the new republic.

The colonists in the New World, although their attention was focused on the virgin territories in the west, remained acutely conscious of the ocean that had afforded them passage to America. While serving as a divider from Europe and as a protective moat, it continued to be their lifeline. For a long time to come Americans would depend on it for manufactured goods to reach them from Europe. Russia, however, lay outside the Atlantic pale and had little to contribute to fill the wants of America.

The Unknown Land

The Atlantic remained also the passageway for any information Americans wanted or needed from abroad. Lacking direct channels of communication with other nations, they remained largely dependent on news reaching them via England, long after they had severed the political ties to their mother country. Until the middle of the nineteenth century American newspapers and magazines acknowledged this frequently by heading foreign reports, especially those from Russia, with the words, "Intelligence Received from London."

It is not hard to understand why the colonists felt little need for

1

firsthand communication with Russia. That country was far removed from America and, indeed, had been a remote country even to Europeans. From antiquity down to modern times Russia has been an enigma to the Western world. Situated at the outer fringes of Europe, geographically, culturally, and politically, she appeared to her curious neighbors a strange and sometimes forbidding land. During most of her history she was either unfriendly or entirely closed to the West. As a result it was difficult for her neighbors to gain knowledge of conditions in that vast country and to acquire understanding of its people and its problems.

As early as the fifth century B.C. Herodotus had reported on the xenophobia of the Scythians, inhabitants of the southern region of what was to become Russia.[2] Their eventual successors, the Slavs, maintained a similar attitude for many centuries. During the Middle Ages, however, strong ties were formed between Russia and Europe, and even closer relations were established between Russia and the Byzantine Empire during the eleventh and twelfth centuries. The Tatar invasions of Russia, in the thirteenth century, caused these to be broken. It was not until after the withdrawal of the Tatars that Russia reemerged on the European horizon, in the early sixteenth century. But the end of the Tatar rule in Russia occurred almost at the time of the discovery of the New World by the Western nations. Because of this historical coincidence the eyes of Europe were turned west just when Russia and her European neighbors could have moved closer to each other.

Furthermore, Russia's own, much more immediate interests barred her from participating in Europe's push beyond the Atlantic. With her aspirations and ambitions leaning in the opposite direction, Russia accelerated the penetration of the East that traders had begun in the Middle Ages. This eastward expansion gathered momentum during the sixteenth century, and it culminated, by the middle of the seventeenth, with the arrival of the Russians at the Pacific.

These movements in opposite directions notwithstanding, numerous reports show that in the sixteenth century England had an extensive commercial intercourse with Russia and thereby greater knowledge than other European nations about conditions in that country. In the next century, when Russian mistrust of foreigners reasserted itself and English merchants were no longer permitted by the Muscovite rulers to visit the interior of the country, information available to the English decreased.[3] But a significant English interest in Russia persisted even after the colonies in America had drawn a good deal of England's commercial activities across the Atlantic. It grew, of course, after Peter the Great opened his country to the West in the beginning of the eighteenth century.

America's interest in Russia and knowledge of the country were bound to be less significant than that of Europe, especially of England. Speaking of political and commercial matters, Thomas Paine could justifiably conclude his remarks on Russia by saying that she appeared to him "excluded from the possibility of rivalling America."[4]

There was a rivalry, however, that concerned Americans during the nation's early years. This was the antagonism toward Europe and its traditions, an antagonism that represented a factor in the development of the American national identity. Though remaining within the sphere of the European culture, Americans were constantly comparing their newly founded national existence with the Old World. In becoming Americans the descendants of Europeans felt compelled to reject the world of their fathers. The historian Cushing Strout, when tracing the development and history of the American image of the Old World, began his narrative by stating that "for much of their history Americans have defined themselves through a deeply felt sense of conflict with Europe."[5] At the same time, however, they acknowledged their European heritage as one of the basic components of their existence. Europe, said Philip Rahv, "served the native [American] imagination both as myth and a reality."[6]

This attitude is reflected in the American version of the "grand tour," which, following the English fashion, was adopted by Americans in the nineteenth century.[7] Its standard itinerary included England, France, especially Paris, and Italy. Side trips to Switzerland, perhaps also to Germany and Holland, were optional. This tour served a twofold purpose for Americans who could afford it: it satisfied a need to acknowledge their European roots and, antithetically, a desire to affirm their own, separate identity by experiencing European customs and habits as alien. Returning home meant reliving the emigration of their ancestors and turning to the new and better world of their children. A popular writer, Samuel Griswold Goodrich, wrote in 1828 in the preface to a children's book on travels in Europe that "in Europe . . . education has trained the people from their youth, to despotic systems. We who are the *protestants* against kings and princes, should fortify ourselves by strong bulwarks, laid deep and early in the minds of our children." And he ended his tales by affirming that, having seen many countries, "I had seen no country where the people were so happy, none that I could love so well, as my own."[8]

Russia was not included in this love-hate relationship. Not having been a part of the main body of European culture, she appeared to American eyes not as a factor in their image of Europe. Americans who ventured to Russia found a country even more alien than the unfamiliar world of Europe. In 1780, Francis Dana, the first official American representative in Russia, found his stay in such alien surroundings a most unsettling experience, a sentiment that was to be echoed by later American travelers. In 1841 the historian John L. Motley, then a secretary to the legation at St. Petersburg, noted in his diary: "The more I see of other countries, the more I like America."[9]

Such an uneasiness did not deter a good number of Americans from visiting Russia when, about the middle of the nineteenth century, political and military developments drew increased attention to the country. In the spring of 1856, as the Crimean War between Russia and the allied powers of England, France, and Turkey came to a close, the *New York Herald* suggested Russia be included in the grand tour: "With the proclamation of the pacification of the Continent, the temptations to our summer birds of passage for a trip to Constantinople and the Crimea, or to Helsingfors, Cronstadt and St. Petersburg, in addition to the old beaten tracks of Germany, the Alps and Italy, will be almost irresistible."[10]

Toward the end of the nineteenth century, American travelers began to reach Russia in greater numbers, and firsthand reports were published with increasing frequency.[11] Diplomats, politicians, journalists, writers, explorers, businessmen, geologists, and plain sightseers set about offering the stay-at-homes accounts of life in Russia.

Characteristically enough, the pragmatic American visitor sought to reflect his fleeting as well as his profound impressions, his observations of the superficial and his speculation on the fundamental, his sense of the latent and of the obvious of Russian existence, his perception of the yesterday, today, and tomorrow of the people, their transient habits and their enduring qualities.

Such personal accounts are a far cry from European efforts to record comprehensive descriptions and analyses of Russia and its people.[12] Only during the years preceding World War I did American scholars begin to evince more than a slight interest in Russia.[13] In 1918 the historian Joseph Kerner could say with a great deal of justification that "we in America, though always cherishing a platonic interest in Russia, because of the similarity of our problems, have really known very little about the Slavs."[14] More recently Erik Erikson, writing about the social significance of childhood in Russia, concluded that "it is difficult . . . to learn much about Russia that is certain, relevant, and articulate at the same time."[15]

Encounters and Confrontations

It was not for lack of formal relations between the governments of the two countries that Russia remained for so long a relatively unknown land to the people of the United States. Some dealings on the official level were started soon after the birth of the new republic. These relations, though tenuous at the beginning, grew more significant as both countries played an ever-expanding role in world politics. The various phases of this relationship have been studied and analyzed by a number of American historians.[16] In this connection the work of the German historian Erwin Hölzle[17] is of special interest because of his thesis that Russia and the United States entered the arena of world politics as incipient superpowers and eventual contenders, each with aspirations going beyond its national borders and with claims permeated by a global messianism.

That it was a European scholar who labored on speculations of this kind, is not surprising. As a consequence of the rise of Russia and the United States, Europe ultimately lost its pivotal position in the world balance of power. The drive in opposite directions that had begun in seventeenth-century Europe, prepared the way for an encounter between the United States and Russia in the Far East, where their territorial ambitions and their economic interests were eventually to clash. In addition, the two countries came to confront each other on the European continent. As a result, the whole northern globe and, finally, the whole world, was drawn into their respective spheres of interests. According to Hölzle, the emergence of the two powers on the international scene thus meant the beginning of the era of global politics that after World War II led to a world-wide confrontation and a period of bipolarity.

Occasional contacts between Russia and America took place long before the founding of the United States. In 1698 William Penn arranged to meet Peter the Great in England to discuss his ideas for a peaceful Europe. It may not be wrong to assume that Penn's American experiment, his Pennsylvania colony, played a significant part in their conversations.[18] People of less prominence met when hunters and traders arrived at the straits between Siberia and the American continent. The question whether there existed a common border between Asia and America, led Peter, in 1724, to order an expedition to proceed east until it should reach a settlement such as that of William Penn. Under the command of Vitus Bering it reached the shores of Alaska in 1728. In 1785, in Catherine's reign, Russians established in Alaska their first settlement, of which no report reached the United States in the east. Finally, in 1799, the czarist government put its official stamp of approval on the private Russian colonizing efforts on the northwestern coast of the American continent by granting special privileges to the Russo-American Company, a Russian trading company.

The fateful results that have since occurred from the American-Russian encounter make an ironic contrast to the inauspicious, almost casual beginnings of their official acquaintance. As early as 1776, when the American revolutionists were looking for support from any quarter, it was planned to send an ambassador to the court of Catherine the Great. But this plan could not be implemented because of the friendly relations existing at the time between Russia and England.[19] In 1780, however, Catherine issued her determined declaration in favor of the freedom of the seas and of armed neutrality. This declaration was obviously directed against the strong English navy rather than the weaker navies of the rebellious colonies and their allies, France and Spain. Accordingly, the Continental Congress interpreted it as a rebuke to England and held that the time was right for establishing relations with Russia. An American representative, by exploiting the tension between Russia and England, was to obtain from Catherine the recognition of the new republic and the signing of a treaty of friendship and peaceful commerce.

The man selected for this objective was Francis Dana, a stolid New Englander. Because he spoke no French, a severe impediment in the diplomatic game he was expected to play, he asked his friend John Adams to allow his French-speaking fourteen-year-old son John Quincy, to accompany him as his secretary. It was this unequal pair that opened the era of diplomatic relations between Russia and the United States.

The mission failed. Imperial Russia was hardly about to deal with a rebellious colony so long as the outcome of the struggle for independence remained in the balance. After cooling his heels at the Russian court for two fruitless years, Dana happily returned to his beloved New England. He had accomplished nothing and had learned little that might have been useful to his country's later diplomatic endeavors. To his young secretary, however, the assignment was in the nature of an apprenticeship to a diplomatic career. In the course of that career, some twenty-seven years later, he came back to the court of St. Petersburg as the first accredited United States minister.

Even after the colonists triumphed and were accorded official recognition by England, Russia continued to withhold formal acknowledgment of the new country. Her reluctance to take this step was due to her desire to avoid English retaliation by interference with Russia's designs in the Middle East. But the political consequences following from the French revolutionary period, which began in 1789, and the Napoleonic Wars eventually brought about Russia's official recognition. The antagonism between France and England and the resulting continental blockade made both Russia and the United States aware of their mutual interests in neutrality and the safety of their maritime commerce. In 1809, six years after the first American consul, Leavitt Harris, had arrived in St.

Petersburg, Russia finally received John Quincy Adams as the American envoy. Able to establish friendly personal relations with the reigning czar, Alexander I, Adams maintained the cordiality that Alexander and President Jefferson had established by frequent correspondence.

In 1812 relations between the United States and Russia were complicated by Napoleon's Russian campaign and the war between the United States and England, Napoleon's archenemy. Russia wanted that war to end in order to obtain England's help against France and, therefore, offered her services for mediating between the United States and England.

By the end of the European wars in 1814, Russia had become a dominant power in European affairs, while the United States was able to pursue her ambitions in her own hemisphere. But the two powers that had emerged on the eastern and western flanks of Europe, were soon to confront each other. Russian advances on the coasts of Oregon and California and, particularly, Russian support of Spain against the South American revolutions appeared to threaten the incipient United States hegemony in the Western Hemisphere. The Monroe Doctrine of 1823, which warned the European powers against interference in the Western Hemisphere, was directed against Russia, leader of the Holy Alliance of European monarchies, more than its other members.

After the potential threat in South America had been thwarted and, in 1824, the line of influence in Alaska and the mutual fishing and trading interests of the United States and Russia in the American northwest settled and agreed upon, the tension between the two powers abated. In 1832, the two countries concluded a treaty of commerce and friendship, notwithstanding the agitation caused in America by the Polish rebellion against Russia of 1830. Also the European revolutions of 1848–1849, in which the conservative Holy Alliance was ranged against liberal forces on the continent, caused a great deal of excitement in the United States but no real antagonism against Russia, because no vital American interests were affected.

The relative stability of the period was utilized by both protagonists to strengthen their footholds in Asia. Neither Perry's coup of 1853, by which the United States forestalled a Russian move to land in Japan, nor contending policies on the Asiatic continent during the following years, represented a serious threat to their relations.

During the Crimean War of 1853–1856, the United States maintained official neutrality. Again no immediate American interests were involved. But this did not prevent the United States from sympathizing with Russia. After all, the victorious Anglo-French coalition could become a danger to American ambitions for greater power, especially in the Western Hemisphere, where both France and England had possessions and interests.

When the American Civil War ensued, this sympathy was repaid by Russia. With England favoring the South, Russia was the only one of the great powers to stand on the side of the Union. The unexplained appearance of the Russian fleet in the New York harbor in 1863 was accepted as a sign of Russian support. At the same time the Unionists pointed to Russia's abolition of serfdom in 1861 as paralleling the Union's endeavors to abolish slavery. Understandably, another Polish rebellion against Russia in 1863 produced little reaction in the war-torn United States, although its aims corresponded to American political ideals.

A zenith in American-Russian relations was reached in 1867 by the purchase of Alaska. The Russian decision to sell their unprofitable holdings in America was influenced by animosity against England. For the United States the acquisition meant another step forward on the road to manifest destiny. It presaged an intensification of the United States' drive to become a Pacific power. As a result of this drive, the United States' interests in that region openly clashed with those of Russia during the entire period that followed the Alaska Purchase and ended with World War I. The slogan of the United States' so-called traditional friendship with Russia was finally abandoned by a more realistic appraisal of United States' interests. This led to an openly anti-Russian position during the Russo-Japanese War of 1904–1905 and an unfriendly attitude toward Russia during the subsequent peace negotiations at Portsmouth, New Hampshire. The treatment of political prisoners in Siberia and of Russian Jews, particularly those holding United States passports, had contributed to the estrangement. When in 1911 the United States abrogated the commercial treaty of 1832, American relations with Russia reached their lowest point.

In 1917, World War I brought the two countries together again, though for a very short time. During the war years Americans attempted to establish bases for a true and lasting friendship and alliance between the two countries. Behind the façade of the autocratic czarist regime they believed to recognize the essentially democratic character of the Russian people and of its local institutions and hoped for liberal reforms. By closer economic cooperation Americans expected both countries to prosper and looked forward to profitable business relations. These hopes rose with the establishment of the short-lived parliamentary regime in February 1917. They ended abruptly in the blaze of the Russian October Revolution, which ushered in the communist rule.

Three factors seem to have determined American-Russian relations from their very start until about the time of the Alaska Purchase: the geographical distance, the absence of conflicting vital interests, and finally, the relationship of each toward England. Time and again friendship or antagonism toward England decided the position that one country would assume toward the other. When they saw that power as their common rival, they moved closer together. But their friendship waned whenever one of them found it advantageous to seek a rapprochement with England. As a consequence "Russo-American relations were usually most cordial when one or the other of the two countries was at odds with England. At such times the nation involved was always more amenable to any requests of the other; while when one of them was making advances to Great Britain it immediately became more indifferent toward the other."[20] In fact, whenever they needed a common front against England and their own territorial expansion was leading them to a possible confrontation, it was usually Russia that yielded to the United States in order to preserve their joint position.[21]

The Popular Image

The official relations between two governments are one thing. Quite another are the feelings that the individuals of one nation harbor toward the people of the other. According to the historian Walter Lacqueur, "it is comparatively easy to write diplomatic history, especially after the opening of the archives; the whole traffic of notes, memoirs, and meetings takes place in a small world of professionals and can be retraced with reasonable accuracy. The image of another nation is something far more complex and elusive."[22]

Opinions held by the citizenry usually defy exact analysis and measurement. The anonymous masses have no authoritative spokesman to articulate their views. Published reports by private individuals are not a reliable standard for the attitude of the general public. Moreover, commonly only a small minority of the people will express their image of another nation. It is certainly possible that the image held by the general public is quite different from that of the relatively few individuals who express it. If it is true, as stated by a scholar who studied English antagonism toward Russia during the period from 1815 to 1841, that "inarticulate opinion can exert at best a negative influence over events" and that "it is articulate sentiment which counts and virtually all such opinion, that of statesmen as well as that of the public,"[23] there is reason to hope that a more or less accurate image can be determined. On the other hand, it was pointed out by Peter G. Filene, in his study of American attitudes toward Soviet Russia, that we may be necessarily limited to "the attitudes of those who are most powerful, or noisy, or educated, or fanatic, rather than most representative," and that, therefore, we are dealing only with "an excerpt from the total reality."[24]

Whatever the "total reality," once an image of a people or country exists in the minds of another, it becomes part of that reality and exerts its own influence. History has been said to consist not only of facts but also of what people thought about them. Accordingly, a national image is as much part and parcel of history as the unfolding of the political and diplomatic relations. Such an image may be merely a faint shadow or an imaginary vision of the objective reality, yet, according to Otto Kirchheimer, who may have been thinking of Plato's allegorical prisoners in the dark cave as well as of the ideological superstructure in Marxist theory, "shadows become substance when they affect people's minds."[25] Indeed, the effects of shadows can be more enduring than those of verifiable facts and factors.

For reasons of geographical distance and different social, political, and cultural developments, the relationship between the United States and Russia provided an especially fertile soil for the growth of stereotypes. Moreover, factors connected with the background of American history and development gave the American image of Russia and the Russians a particular coloring. The effect of Enlightenment rationalism, which had made a strong imprint on the men of the American Revolution and the postrevolutionary generations, showed up in two conflicting ways: on the one hand, Americans were animated by an unquestioning belief in progress and the perfectibility of man and society—hence the call for revolutionary change; on the other, they believed in permanence, stability, balance, and the rule of law.[26] As a consequence of this dichotomy, the violent contrast between the extremes of wealth and poverty that they found in Russia, and the lack of commercial and industrial initiative in that seemingly stagnant and archaic country, outraged the Americans' quest for progress and modernization. At the same time, the confusing forms of Russian societal life and the unforeseeable developments that could emerge from the depths of its seething populations were experienced as a threat to the middle-class need for stability and security.

In addition, the Puritan component of their heritage led Americans to adopt frequently a moralistic view of many Russian conditions, while their steadily rising economic power found its expression in a feeling of superiority and in nationalistic views. This nationalism took at times the form of a virulent racism.[27] Americans considered themselves the junior branch of the supposedly superior Anglo-Saxon community, with England the leading member. Toward the turn of the nineteenth century, when the leadership began to pass into the hands of the more zestful Americans, many American writers and politicians loudly proclaimed Anglo-Saxon, that is American, racial superiority as a foundation of their claims to global predominance. They were undecided whether the Russians were to be counted among the inferior peoples, although many expressed that thought by calling them Asiatics or Asiatics with a European veneer.

Whatever the American image of Russia during the period from 1775 to 1917, its study is made possible because many opinions were preserved in print. Books, magazines, newspapers, private papers, constitute an almost endless source of material from which opinions can be drawn and distilled. These opinions range over a wide field and pass judgments on countless facts and facets of Russian life.

The record seems to show that there were five groups of questions on Russia and the Russians that were raised and answered by Americans throughout the period: the Russian national character; the state and relative height of Russian civilization; the Russian political system; Russia's position in world politics; and the relationship to and comparison with the United States. This is not to say that the opinions that were expressed, nor the selections included in this volume, fall always neatly into one of these groups. To the contrary, a man may have spoken his mind on various of these questions. But establishing such categories may permit us to gain a better perspective of the views on Russia held by Americans. Beyond that it must be left to the reader's own imagination to extract or deduce from some of the opinions the outlines—however rough and imperfect one must expect these to be—of the total picture.

The National Character

The first question, that of the national character, arises almost inevitably when one people looks at another. It is simply an attempt to determine the type of people with whom one is confronted, their attributes, their strengths and weaknesses as human beings, their "good" and their "bad" qualities. When describing Russian character traits, Americans usually proceeded from the controversial assumption that the Russians, indeed all peoples, possessed definable, distinguishing characteristics. They stated as truth what they believed they saw, and were hardly deterred by such reservations as the extent of their acquaintance with the country and its people. Frequently they simply repeated what they understood to be the traditional view of the Russian national character. The image thus formed or accepted represented to them the reality, and it is, of course, this image that appears in their opinions.[28]

Not all Americans, when speaking of the Russians, considered the multinational character of the country. Those who did, usually referred in their observations to the Great Russians, or "true Russians," to Ukrainians, Cossacks, Siberian settlers, and so forth. As a rule, the national traits observed among the Great Russians, and possibly among their close neighbors, White Russians and Ukrainians, were recognized as *the* Russian national character traits. This approach is understandable because these groups were numerically, culturally, and politically dominant.

Throughout the whole period under review, the great mass of the Russian people belonged to the peasantry. The middle class was as yet very small. The industrial proletariat, which even in 1917 accounted for only a low percentage of the total population, had not yet shed all vestiges of its peasant origin. Urban workers were difficult to distinguish from their peasant fathers and brothers. The moujik was, therefore, often seen as the average Russian.

The complaint of Alexis de Tocqueville, that no visitors to Russia pay any attention to the lower classes—"the only thing which is at all interesting or has any dignity"[29]—could not be made so definitely about American visitors. That the Russian peasantry represented a social and cultural group unlike any in America was one more reason why the eyes of not a few Americans fastened upon it and why opinions on the Russian character were frequently derived from acquaintance with that class. But the responses were often confusing and contradictory. Some Americans were moved to sympathy by the lot of the downtrodden peasants. They traced their deplorable state to the socioeconomic conditions under which they were living, and were inclined to look at the peasants in a favorable light. In 1792, the *New York Magazine* called the peasant "the hereditary victim of avarice and oppression. . . . Indolence and inertion are the consequences, and he scarcely soars in mental endowment above the humiliating level of irrational creation." The same article, however, called "the national character . . . far from being savage and even unamiable."[30]

Others preferred to ignore the disquieting social and economic circumstances and to portray the peasantry as a happy-go-lucky breed. As late as 1904, a visiting clergyman, Moncure Daniel Conway, a friend of the diplomat Eugene Schuyler, wrote:

. . . there was unconscious poverty . . . but no squalor, no violence, and no painful scenes. The Russian peasantry impressed me as the happiest I had ever seen in any country. And there is nothing better than happiness. They have each their parcel of land, untaxed, and perfect freedom. They have their Sunday festivals and dances, no anxieties about their souls, and no politics to divide and excite them. They have their pretty sweethearts and wives. They have no strikes, no ambitions. Ignorant they may be, in a bookish sense, but how many bookish people are ignorant of things known to these humble folk, who live among their fruits and their harvests, bees and birds?[31]

Americans who had access to the upper levels of Russian society or were impressed by social status stressed the qualities of self-sacrifice, religiosity, loyalty, and obedience of the masses. Entrance into court circles, often the culmination of a visit to Russia, induced some visitors to see the country and its situation in a more optimistic light and to disregard less glamorous aspects of Russian social life.

It is not only among Americans that one finds the upper class harboring a sympathetic attitude toward the upper class of another country, accompanied by a disregard of obvious social ills and an indifferent position toward its lower classes. The same charge has been lodged against certain French writers of upper-class background who early in the nineteenth century wrote about Russian conditions. Their reports were said to be influenced by their extensive contacts with the Russian nobility.[32] Tocqueville called this a general phenomenon originating from conditions of social inequality: "The same man who is full of humanity towards his fellow creatures when they are at the same time his equals becomes insensible to these afflictions as soon as that equality ceases. His mildness should therefore be attributed to the equality of conditions rather than to civilization and education."[33]

It can be said, however, that many of the American visitors to Russia reported their observations without catering to prejudices derived from the rank and social privilege of the higher circles of Russian society. Whatever the bases for their judgments, the observations reported by Americans on Russian character traits do not seem to have varied greatly during the period from the beginning of the American Revolution in 1775 to the Russian Revolution in 1917.

Not necessarily consistent, they more often than not saw the Russian people as simple, natural, emotional, sensual, impulsive, impressionable, reckless, generous, improvident, cheerful, polite, melancholy, fatalistic, unreflective, imitative, passive, docile, servile, resourceful, and courageous.

On the whole, these observations were more favorable than adverse, more sympathetic than antagonistic. Yet, in 1950, the historian Thomas Bailey concluded that nineteenth-century Americans had "most commonly" spoken of negative traits such as "anti-foreignism, secretiveness, suspicion, duplicity, evasiveness, procrastination, crudeness, callousness, ruthlessness and brutality." He also mentioned resignation to absolutism, dependence on bureaucrats and centralized authority, toleration of censorship and secret police, the Oriental attributes of patience and docility ("scratch a Russian and you will find a Tatar"), expansionist and imperialist tendencies, and the missionary drive of Pan-Slavism.[34] Bailey had been studying the encounters and confrontations of the United States and Russia in the diplomatic field, and thus his conclusions were largely based upon diplomatic and other official papers. Moreover, his studies were made during the period of the cold war, a fact that may have had an influence on his findings. In any case, one cannot expect to discover complete unanimity of American opinions about the Russian national character, but must be satisfied with establishing their preponderant tenor.

Analysis of the traits attributed by the members of one group to those of another enables one to draw conclusions also about the people who formulated the opinions. In our case, Americans saw the Russians as a people characterized by a passive disposition. This emphasis on the Russians' inactive and unreflective nature leaves the impression that a dynamic, practical-minded people had been looking at their temperamental opposites.

Frequently, feelings of superiority are present when a more active group tries to judge another considered more passive. Similar, patronizing sentiments prevail when individuals of prosperous background look at a group viewed as socially or economically inferior. One notices such latent feelings of superiority when one reads American reports on Russian character traits, even though their tone is sympathetic. Perhaps one may qualify Tocqueville's comment by pointing out that men who minimize the economic afflictions of socially lower groups may try to assuage their feelings of guilt by granting their inferiors attributes of positive nature. Another reason for the generally favorable evaluation of the Russian character may be found in similarities that were presumed to exist between the United States and Russia: the relative youth of both nations in terms of their appearance on the world scene; their freedom from the formal manners and constraining customs of the old Europe; a pioneering spirit combined with territorial expansion; physical similarities of much of the countryside; and the existence of serfdom in Russia and of slavery in the United States and their abolition at about the same time.

Russian Civilization

Beginning with George Washington,[35] most Americans, notwithstanding their granting the Russians character traits of a predominantly positive nature, looked upon the Russian society as one of barbarians or semibarbarians. In 1814, *Niles' Weekly Register*, one of the best-known American weeklies of the early nineteenth century,[36] wrote: "The world cannot furnish a body of people more ignorant, more brutal, more slavish." It was conceded, though, that the Russians were making progress in matters of civilization and in education. Their religion made them part of Christendom, but due to the seemingly strange forms of their Orthodox religion and worship they were often considered Christians in name only. Some Americans, as well as some Europeans, who feared the pressure of the Orient and of the Mohammedan Turks upon Christian Europe, praised Russia as the eastern bulwark of Western civilization. Religious bias, however, played its own role in this connection. Some Protestant clerics saw in Russia a defender against Catholicism and popery, and, if conservative, a protector against the tide of liberal ideas. Charles Brandon Boynton, a Protestant clergyman, wrote in 1856:

> Protestant and Russian civilizations *may* yet affiliate, and the government of the North [Russia] be liberalized, not by association with an

infidel democracy [England], but by the spirit of Protestant freedom. . . . A Sclavonic civilization, Atheism and the Papacy are the real contending powers in Europe. With which should America sympathize?[37]

Roman Catholics biased against Protestant England also spoke favorably of Russia. "Russia for the last hundred and fifty years and more has really been fighting the battles of Christendom against the followers of the Prophet, in continuation of the old Crusades preached by the Popes," asserted Orestes Augustus Brownson, an American Catholic writer, in 1854 during the Crimean War. At the same time he reproached Catholic France, ally of Protestant England, as having been "false to her mission."[38] This is not to say that most American Catholics did not continue to see the Russian Orthodox belief as a heresy. When in the 1870s the czarist regime was torn by internal strife, the *American Catholic Quarterly Review* called for "replacement of shallow superstition by true religion" and for religious liberty and public freedom to lead Russia "from the dark ages of Asiatic barbarity," as represented by czarism and its official church, to "Christian civilization."[39]

The question whether Russia was part of Europe or Asia was for a long time a subject of intense discussion between Russians and their European neighbors. These debates, which produced numerous publications of historical, political, and philosophical nature, served essentially as a means of self-identification for both sides.[40] Americans had little wish or need to participate in this passionate dialogue because the answer meant nothing to them as far as their identity as a nation was concerned. Those Americans who did stress the Oriental character of Russia and her people, were implying that Russian civilization was on a lower order than that of Western Europe and certainly not equal to their own. This negative judgment may bear some relation to their benevolent view of the Russian national character. In acknowledging with condescending generosity the basic though not always obvious virtues of the moujik, they tacitly pointed to the distance that existed in their eyes between the high level of their own civilization, based as it were, on rational values, and the more rudimentary forms of Russian life, remnants of archaic traditions and the products of seemingly irrational forces.

The nature of the Russian government presented another barrier to understanding. Very often no distinction is made between the acts of a foreign government and the actions of the people subject to that government. That the Russians themselves were the chief victims of the repression and that at times the government, for its own purposes, encouraged violence by some segments of the population, was ignored. As a result, attributes such as "brutal," "barbarous," and "uncivilized" were often applied to the people when they should have been used to characterize the procedures and policies of the government.

The Autocracy

The Government of Russia is entirely despotical the Souvereign is absolute in all the extent of the word, the persons the estates the fortunes of the nobility depend entirely upon his Caprice. And the nobility have the same power over the people, that the Souvereign has over them. The Nation is wholly composed of Nobles & Serfs or in other words of Masters and Slaves.

These are thoughts put down on paper by John Quincy Adams at the beginning of American-Russian diplomatic relations, when he was fourteen years old.[41]

A century later the young Woodrow Wilson, long before he became president, voiced a different opinion:

There can be no reasonable doubt that the power of Russia's Czar, vast and arbitrary as it seems, derives its strength from the Russian people. It is not the Czar's personal power; it is his power as head of the national church, as semi-sacred representative of the race and its historical development and organization. Its roots run deep into the tenacious, nourishing soil of immemorial habit. The Czar represents history, not a caprice.[42]

Wilson changed his view when the czarist government was overthrown in the February Revolution of 1917. He then denounced czarism as "Oriental" in origin and foreign to Russian democratic heritage.[43] His first view, however, and the antithetical remarks made by the young Adams are characteristic of the contradictory attitudes Americans adopted toward the Russian autocratic system throughout the whole period we are covering.

For this reason, the assertion made by George F. Kennan in 1956 —that "interest in Russia among the American public has been confined to a sympathetic following of the struggle against autocracy"[44]—is not borne out by the facts. On the contrary, there were at all times Americans who stressed the good aspects of czarism and its supposed advantages for the Russian people while playing down the oppressive character of the system. There were those such as Henry Middleton, American minister to Russia from 1820 to 1830, who considered the autocracy necessary for the survival of the Russian state, although they were aware of the need for reforms.[45] Other diplomats were more unreservedly ready to condone a system that they, the official representatives of a democratic government, should have abhorred. James Buchanan, president of the United States from 1857 to 1861, wrote in 1833, when he was American minister to Russia: "The most ardent Republican, after having resided here for one year, would be clearly convinced that the great mass of people, composed as it is of ignorant and superstitious barbarians, who are also slaves, is not fit for political freedom. Besides they are perfectly contented."[46]

Apologists for the czarist regime sought to justify it because of the Russian national character, the lack of political maturity of the population, or on the basis of Russian history. Many called attention to traditional liberties and immunities existing on the local level, such as the *mir*, the peasant commune, which they saw as democratic institutions within the autocracy. They overlooked, however, the fact that such local freedom as was available to the moujik, was essentially secured by his poverty, his marginal existence within a vast country lacking communications and an efficient government machinery. The great distances afforded protection against the central government as well as, according to Madame de Staël, prevented "the despotism of the nobles from bearing heavily upon the people in everyday affairs."[47] His lack of possessions, therefore, gave the peasant a certain, though limited amount of freedom—

hence, the old saying that where there is nothing to get, the emperor has lost his rights. But it seems that the moujik was not without desires for more extensive and more meaningful liberties. And once he was "given a taste for freedom developed an appetite for more."[48] In time many individual Americans recognized and celebrated this longing for political and social advancement. Others could have learned a lesson from the fledgling diplomat, John Quincy Adams, who, in 1783, after his return from Russia, wrote to his mother "on the esteem they have for liberty, even when one would think they should not know that such a thing exists."[49]

Even many of those who defended the regime, stressed the advantages of democratic government and hoped for a change for the better in the future. The question was only whether the change would come legally and gradually or whether a revolution was unavoidable.

Generally, the possibility of violent revolution came to people's minds when Russia was beset by internal crises. It was first mentioned by Americans around the time of and after the Decembrist Conspiracy of 1825, when a group of young men, mostly officers of aristocratic background, plotted to obtain a liberal constitution. The thought of revolution in Russia recurred during the European revolutions of 1848–1849, and during and after the Crimean War. In the 1870s the nihilist agitation and assaults and the brutal suppression of the terrorist movement again brought about the feeling that such a crisis existed. And, of course, during the events of 1905 and 1906, the defeat of Russia by Japan and the revolutionary disturbances that followed, it became a commonplace to speculate about revolution in Russia. Carl Schurz wrote about it in 1900,[50] and the conservative Henry Adams expected the worst when he wrote in 1904: "I am half crazy with fear that Russia is sailing straight into another French revolution which may upset all Europe and us too. A serious disaster to Russia might smash the whole civilized world. Other people see only the madness; I see only the ruin. Russia is completely off her head."[51]

It may have been the wish for moderation that led some people even on the eves of the revolutions of 1905 and 1917 to state that there was no such danger. Such was the attitude, in 1905, of Andrew

Dickson White, who had been minister to Russia in 1892–1894: "Revolution in Russia? There will be no revolution. . . . The peasantry is little above the brute. It would be just as unreasonable to expect wild cattle on the plains to revolt against the cowboys as to expect the Russian peasants to revolt against the autocracy."[52] In 1916 the lawyer, diplomat, and novelist Richard Washburn Child exclaimed: "No, not revolution. . . . Something less dramatic is in store for Russia. Business! . . . It is business which will be able to force liberalism on Russia. And it will do this not by revolution but by evolution."[53]

Russia as a World Power

The autocracy not only overwhelmed the Russian masses. It also served to accentuate Russia's military power abroad, which, in the wake of Napoleon's final defeat in 1815, cast terrifying shadows over Europe. Napoleon himself expressed repeatedly his fear that "the barbarians of the North will possess Europe." The Comte de las Cases, his companion in exile at St. Helena, reports him as saying:

> Who can avoid shuddering at the thought of such a vast mass, unassailable on the flanks or in the rear, ascending upon us with impunity; if triumphant, overwhelming everything in its course, or, if defeated, retiring amidst the cold and desolation, that may be called its forces of reserve, and possessing every faculty for issuing forth at a future opportunity.[54]

Throughout the nineteenth century fear of Russia was general in Europe[55] in view of the predominance she had gained during and after the Napoleonic Wars. This fear was expressed particularly within liberal and republican groups. Conservatives generally welcomed her influence in Europe, seeing her as a shield against the rising forces of liberalism and the movement toward popular rule. Although Russia's defeat in the Crimean War demonstrated serious internal weaknesses, the unfavorable impressions caused by the debacle were soon tempered by her rapid recovery.

Russia had been recognized as a military power in Europe since the Seven Years' War (1756–1763), when her troops, for the first time, had occupied Berlin. Her economic growth and increasing military strength also impressed knowledgeable Americans. When speaking of this, Americans considered it in relation to their own international position as much as in comparison with the power of European states. In fact, they saw in Russia a potential or actual counterweight against England or France or both. Whenever England and France, the principal powers in Europe, might gain the upper hand over Russia, Americans would side with Russia. Whenever Russia threatened to overpower Central and Western Europe, Americans would take the part of the Western powers. The aim of American policy with regard to Russia was, therefore, the maintenance of a world balance of power.

By the close of the nineteenth century the United States had come into its own as a world power. The old suspicions and prejudices against England had given way to an amicable understanding, one which was to survive the Russian Revolution and two world wars. The traditional policy of cooperation between Russia and the United States—a common front against England whenever that country threatened the interests of either one—had lost its basis. When the last years of the century saw an open clash between the United States and Russia in China, their self-confidence, their growing nationalism and pride in the rise of their commerce and industry, made many Americans belittle Russian strength. Mark Twain's disdainful words expressed the view of a generation that proclaimed an American manifest destiny extending beyond the limits of the Western Hemisphere: "And look at Russia. It spreads all around and everywhere, and yet ain't no more important in this world than Rhode Island is, and hasn't got half as much in it worth saving."[56]

Critical views of Russia's strength had, of course, been voiced by some Americans long before. In 1821, at the seeming height of Russia's position in Europe as the leader of the Holy Alliance, President Monroe had written: "Russia seems at present the great bug-bear of the European politicians on the land. I cannot but think, however, that the future growth of Russia . . . is not a little over-rated."[57] Voices to the contrary were, of course, heard throughout the century. Theodore Roosevelt, the spokesman for the new

American nationalism, expressed the ambiguity in American think-ing about Russia's future position in the world: "Sometimes I do feel inclined to believe that the Russian is the one man with enough barbarous blood in him to be the hope of a world that is growing effete. But I think that this thought comes only when I am reasonably dispirited."[58]

The Great Parallel

Expectation of Russian growth and potential world leadership was probably strengthened by the existence of what, in 1852, the American minister to Russia, Neill S. Brown, had called "a strange superstition" on the part of the Russians.[59] This was their mission-ary belief that theirs was a unique nation differing from all others, and, in fact, superior to the peoples of the West; that they had been divinely chosen to conquer and rule the world; and that to reach that end they must not hesitate to go to the extreme limits of action. Thoughts of this nature, voiced time and again by nineteenth-century Russian writers, were frequently noted by Americans.[60]

Many nations, for that matter, have called themselves chosen peoples, and, in the words of the American historian Russel Blaine Nye, "no nation in modern history has been quite so consistently dominated as the United States by the belief that it has a particular mission in the world, and a unique contribution to make to it."[61]

The missionary claims made by the Russians and the American belief in a manifest destiny originated, however, from different circumstances. America's sense of mission developed from an unbounded optimism, from feelings of power, from a material superiority founded upon a supposedly better concept of social and political organization. In contrast, Russia's sense of mission was largely the product of resentment and frustration. It evolved as Russians compared conditions in their country with those in the West. It was born as a compensatory faith and was fed and kept alive by the striking inadequacies and stinging weaknesses of Russian political and social life.[62] Americans, aware of the great potential of Russia, were bound to be impressed by these Russian assertions voiced, as they were, in desperation and, therefore, sounding perhaps that much more forceful.

Tocqueville's famous prognosis of 1835 expressed another kind of parallelism between the two countries:

> There are at the present time two great nations in the world, which started from different points, but seem to tend towards the same end. I allude to the Russians and the Americans. Both of them have grown up unnoticed; and while the attention of mankind was directed else-where, they have suddenly placed themselves in the front rank among the nations, and the world learned their existence and their greatness at almost the same time. . . . Their starting-point is different and their courses are not the same; yet each of them seems marked out by the will of Heaven to sway the destinies of half the globe.[63]

A similar, less-known prophecy had been made half a century earlier by the German Baron von Grimm, agent of Catherine the Great in France, who wrote to her on December 31, 1790:

> Two empires will . . . divide among themselves all privileges of civili-zation and of intellectual, scientific, military, and industrial power: Russia in the east, and in the west America, so recently freed; and we other peoples in the present center of the world will be too de-graded and humiliated to remember what we once were, except through a vague and stupid tradition.[64]

This remarkable statement, considering the time when it was made, probably reflected a feeling prevalent in European political circles when the French Revolution appeared to spell the doom of the continent.

Americans were at that time not thinking of a possible bipolarity between their country and Russia, although the idea of a parallel situation of the two was already mentioned. Unlike Thomas Paine,[65] Silas Deane, one of the American revolutionary agents in Europe, saw in 1777 a role for Russia in the coming world-power constella-tion equal to that of America. Understandably, England appeared to him still as the center of world power, but he saw her leaning on both America and Russia as secondary powers:

It is easy to foresee that Great Britain, America, and Russia united will command not only Europe but the whole world. Russia, like America, is a new state, and rises with the most astonishing rapidity. Its demands for British manufactures and its supplies of raw materials increase nearly as fast as the American, and when both come to centre in Great Britain, the riches as well as power of that Kingdom will be unparalleled in the annals of Europe, or perhaps of the world. Like a Colossus, with one foot on Russia and the other on America, it will bestride, as Shakespeare says, your poor European world, and the powers which now strut and look big will creep about between its legs to find dishonourable graves.[66]

A few years later J. Hector St. John de Crèvecœur, an American colonial who had returned to France, published in his *Letters from an American Farmer* a comparison presumably made by a Russian visitor to America:

I view the present Americans as the seed of future nations, which will replenish this boundless continent; the Russians may be in some respects compared to you; we likewise are a new people, new. I mean, in knowledge, arts and improvements. Who knows what revolutions Russia and America may one day bring about; we are perhaps nearer neighbours than we imagine.[67]

The juxtaposition of the two powers became more apparent to Americans during the times of the Holy Alliance and the issuance of the Monroe Doctrine in 1823. At that time an American politician and diplomat, Alexander Hill Everett, remarked also on the shift in the world balance of power. He wrote in 1827:

. . . the discovery and colonization of America and the East Indies by Great Britain, and the conquest of the whole north of Asia by Russia, which took place at about the same time, prepared the way for the introduction into the European system of new elements, capable of becoming after a while much superior in weight and importance to the original mass.[68]

Julius Fröbel, a German exile then living in the United States, published in 1855 an article in the *San Francisco Journal* in which he stressed the parallel political rise and development of the United States and Russia. He prognosticated, however, that the rule of the world would be shared between these two powers as well as Western Europe.[69]

In accordance with the official protestations of friendship voiced on both sides and based on their community of interests vis-à-vis England, Americans generally expected their country and Russia to remain friends. By the middle of the nineteenth century, however, many differing voices were heard. In 1872, John Lothrop Motley, the diplomat and historian, spoke of their so-called traditional friendship as "platonic," based as he saw it, "on entire incompatibility of character, absence of sympathy, and a plentiful lack of common interest." But he thought that these ingredients might make for a "more enduring passion" than the presence of sincere affection.[70]

In the last decades of the century, though, when the United States and Russia became contenders on the Asiatic shores of the Pacific, warnings about the consequences of their acutely conflicting interests were issued with ever greater frequency. The conviction that ultimately they would contend for world power captured the minds of many American writers and politicians. The eloquent words about their eternal friendship that had been voiced at the time of the Alaska Purchase, about their common interests that demanded "that they should go hand in hand in their march to empire,"[71] had been forgotten. After the Russo-Japanese War and the revolution in Russia in 1905–1906, the notion of a dangerous bipolarity lost its force on the American mind. It came to life again by the end of World War II.

1 THIS NATION IS FAR FROM BEING CIVILIZED

John Quincy Adams (1767–1848)

It is appropriate to begin with an essay of the fourteen-year-old John Quincy Adams, written about 1781–1782 in St. Petersburg.[72] One of the first persons, certainly the youngest, from the new country across the ocean to set foot on Russian soil, he was probably also the first American to set down on paper his observations and views of the country.

"Master Johnny," as he was called, had already accompanied his father, John Adams, on a mission to France when only ten. From this trip he wrote in 1778 to his mother, Abigail, in his childlike manner:

> Honoured Mamma,—My Pappa enjoins it upon me to keep a journal, or a diary of the Events that happen to me, and of objects that I see, and of Characters that I converse with from day to day; and altho. I am convinced of the utility, importance & necessity of this Exercise, yet I have not patience and perseverance enough to do it so Constantly as I ought. My Pappa who takes a great deal of Pains to put me in the right way, has also advised me to Preserve copies of all my letters, & has given me a Convenient Blank Book for this end; and altho I shall have the mortification a few years hence to read a great deal of my Childish nonsense, yet I shall have the Pleasure and advantage of Remarking the several steps by which I shall have advanced in taste, judgment and knowledge. A journal Book & a letter Book of a Lad of Eleven years old Can not be expected to contain much of Science, Litterature, arts, wisdom, or wit, yet it may serve to perpetuate many observations that I may make, & may hereafter help me to recolect both persons & things that would other ways escape my memory.[73]

Johnny had judged correctly his youthful lack of patience and perseverance. His notebook does not reveal much about what and whom he saw in Russia three years later and practically nothing about events connected with the diplomatic mission of Francis Dana, whom he assisted as secretary and interpreter. But his essay on general conditions in Russia, which follows, sets the tone for many of the opinions on Russia voiced by Americans during the next century and a half. There is the reference to the despotic character of the government structure and the disadvantages of this system for the population, especially the lower classes. Implicit is the comparison with that of the American republic. Stressed is the instability of the Russian political order as the cause of past and future upheavals and the low state of civilization of the country.

Many years later, in 1820, when as secretary of state under President Monroe he issued instructions to the minister to Russia, Henry Middleton, Adams had changed his opinion with respect to the instability inherent in the despotic system. He then called Russia "the only party to the compact [of the Holy Alliance] free from that fermentation which threatens the existence of the rest."[74]

•————————————————————————————•

THE GOVERNMENT of Russia is entirely despotical the Souvereign is absolute in all the extent of the word, the persons the estates the fortunes of the nobility depend entirely upon his Caprice. And the nobility have the same power over the people, that the Souvereign has over them. The Nation is wholly composed of Nobles & Serfs or in other words of Masters and Slaves. The Countryman is attached to the land in which he is born if the land is sold he is sold with it; and he is obliged to give to his Landlord the portion of his time which he chuses to demand it is commonly two days in a week if I am not mistaken. Others make them pay a sort of tax of two or three Roubles a year. This makes a large Revenue for the Landlords if they have a great Number of Serfs. And there are some of the nobles who have an amazing Quantity of them out of each five hundreds they are obliged to furnish one to the Empress every year for the army; this forms her Army: I have been assured from good Authority that there is one Nobleman who furnishes 1300 men a year to the Empress: according to that the number of his slaves would be 650,000. Supposing each of these slaves pays him a Rouble a Year his revenue will be more than 100,000 £ Sterling per Annum. This form of Government is disadvantageous to the Souvereign, to the Nobles and to the People. . . .*

As the Nobles all depend upon the Souvereign: they are always in danger, of their estates being confiscated and themselves sent into Siberia; it is commonly the fate of the favourites: Menzicoff, the Dolgorouki's, Biron, Bestucheff, Osterman, L'Estocq, all these have been the sport of Fortune, for some time. The favourites of the Emperors and then sent to Siberia into exile, there to live in misery. . . . an author† who has written upon Russia says he has seen Lands change Masters three or four times in the Course of year. This is certainly not advantageous for the Nobility and as to the People no body I believe will assert that a People possibly can be happy who are subjected to personal Slavery: Some of these Serfs are immensely rich: but they are not free and therefore they are dispised. besides, they depend still upon the nobles, who make them contribute the more for their riches: a Nobleman wants money; if he has any Serfs; he feuds and lets them know, that he must have a thousand Roubles, (more or less, according to Circumstances) at a certain time; this the Serf has a right to refuse, but in that Case his landlord orders him to go and work upon such a piece of ground: so he is obliged either to give the money, or to go and work. The richer they are, naturally, the more the nobles prize them: thus a Common man costs not more than 80 or 100 Roubles at most (N.B. 1 Rouble is about 4 shillings Sterling) but I have seen a Man who gave to his Landlord for his Liberty and for that of his descendants 450,000 Roubles. This proves how much they esteem

---

* Before explaining this system's disadvantages for the nobility, the young Adams gives an account of four palace revolutions that had occurred in the eighteenth century. He believed that this form of government exposed the ruler to the continual threat of such uprisings within the court itself.—Ed.

† Manstein's Memoirs of Russia—J.Q.A.

their Liberty. . . . The People are kept in the greatest ignorance, and are taught that whatever the Souvereign does or does [not] must be right. So, when they think any thing is very extraordinary they say: "Nobody can tell that but god and the Emperor." They are a [sic] very Superstitious; and revere very strongly all sorts of crucifices, Images of the Virgin Mary, of Saints &c. They carry this much farther than the Roman Catholics, for when they pass before any Church they turn their faces to it, and bow and make the sign of the cross to it for five minutes together. This superstition rather than national bravoury makes the Russians excellent Troops, when they have a good general. for supposing they are upon a march, or upon the point of giving battle, and are short of Provisions, if the general gives them some good Reason and orders them to fast for 40 hours, they will do it very punctually. . . . [The Russian] Code of Laws has always been very imperfect. the present Empress [Catherine the Great] has done a great deal to reduce it to a certainty, and put it in order: but has not as yet entirely succeeded. the Empress often publishes Ukases which have the forces of Laws; but she can annul them when she pleases or her successor may annul them by other Ukases so that properly speaking they are only ordonnances. they however are the only Laws by which the Empire is governed: so absolute is the power of the Souvereign, that instead of being subject to the Laws, the Laws are Subject to him. Upon the whole this Nation is far from being civilized: their Customs, their dress, and even their amusements, are yet gross and barbarous: it is said that in some parts of the Empire, the women think their husbands despise them or don't Love them, if they don't thrash them now & then but I do not give this as a fact: in Petersburg they have bathes, where they go pell-mell men and women. they bathe themselves at first in very warm water, and from thence they plunge themselves into the snow, & roll themselves in it. they accustom themselves to this from Infancy, and they think it preserves them from Scurvy. . . .

2 THE RUSSIANS HAVE FEW MORAL VIRTUES

John Ledyard (1751–1789)

John Ledyard, an adventurer and explorer from Connecticut who had accompanied Captain Cook on his last voyage, sailed, in 1784, for Europe in the hope of enlisting support and obtaining funds for an expedition to the northwestern coast of America. In Paris he was able to find interest and assistance on the part of people such as Thomas Jefferson, Lafayette, and John Paul Jones. But his plan ultimately failed, and he decided to reach the Bering Strait via Russia and Siberia. After Thomas Jefferson tried unsuccessfully to obtain permission for his trip from Catherine II, Ledyard decided to plead his cause in person. He proceeded to Russia from London via Hamburg, Copenhagen, and Stockholm, traversed alone and on foot the frozen Gulf of Bothnia, and arrived after many weeks in St. Petersburg, where he was able to secure the permission of the empress. But local authorities in Siberia detained him and sent him back to St. Petersburg. He was, finally, expelled from Russia as a suspected spy.

Of this trip made in 1787–1788, Ledyard kept a journal, from which the following selection has been excerpted.[75] It shows his unfavorable opinion of the Russians, especially of the lower orders of their society. His expulsion from the country served to confirm his negative judgment of the secular and religious customs of the people as well as their morals. He put the blame, however, not solely on their character but in part, at least, on the political setup of the country.

33

I HAVE OBSERVED from Petersburg to this place [Yakutsk, Siberia], and here more than any where that the Russians in general have few moral Virtues, the body of the people are almost totally without. the Laws of the Country are mostly penal Laws; but all civil Laws are but negative instructors; they inform people what they must not do, and affix no reward to the Virtue: This in some Countries is made the business of Religion & in a few instances of the civil Laws. In this unfortunate Country it is a business of neither civil nor ecclesiastical Concern. A Citizen here fulfils his duty to the Laws if like a base Asiatic he licks the feet of his superior in Rank; & his duty to his God if he adorns his house with a set of ill looking brass or silver Saints & worships them. They have never heard that sweet Truth that virtue is its own Reward & know no more of such an Idea than a New Zealander. It is for this Reason that their Peasantry, in particular are indubitably the most unprincipled in Christendom. I looked for certain Virtues of the heart that are called natural. I find them mot [sic] in the most remote & obscure Villages in the Empire but on the contrary I find the rankest vices to abound as much as in their Capital. . . .

I left Mogaloff on the 18 of March and arrived at the Barrier Town 90 Versts the same evening—waited in the Street half an hour before called in to the Majors—from there conducted to the Directors house—alone in an anti-room there half an hour.—At last the dear moment came that I was conducted over a Bridge across a little River, across the Barrier into the little Village Tolochin in Poland.—O Liberty! O Liberty! how sweet are thy embraces! Having met thee in Poland I shall bless that Country; Indeed I believe it wants the blessing of every charitable mind. I was conducted for quarters to the house of a Jew. not being permitted to enter the Dominions of a people more destitute of principle than themselves they hover about its boundaries here in great numbers. It was a large dirty house filled with dirt & noise & children. When my Baggage was brought in, I found I had been robbed of 5 Roubles that were in a Bag in my Portmanteau. I discovered it to the Russian Lieutenant who instantly set about seeking for it. It was found in the Boots of the Russian Postillion, & as the Russian Soldier was Guard over me & my Property & was drunk, at the moment (tho' not before) I suspected him to be an accomplice. I wrote so in my letter to General Passek. The Russian Officer did me the Satisfaction, without asking or thinking of it myself, to strip & flog the Postillion before me. Thus was my Voyage in Russia finished as it was begun. I was robbed at Moscow on my setting out of 50 Roubles, which I lost entirely, & from that time to this at different times whether in Russia or Siberia I have constantly had something stolen from me. For the third time only since my confinement I slept without my Clothes this Night. . . .

I this Morning quitted my Russ Conductors. . . . In the other parts of my Voyage the transition has been so gentle from the different Characters of People different to each other that I sometimes lost the Gradations. A second visit to the same places has convinced me of the Error & I have as well as I could rectified it. There also were others quite abrupt but none of them were so when I compared to the change I mark to day in entering the Dominions of the late King of Prussia: on the Confines of every other Kingdom there has been a Melange of Character of considerable extent within each, forming a kind of Suburb. It has not been so to day I have within the Space of 3 English Miles leapt the great barrier of Asiatic & European manners; from Servility, Indolence, Filth, Vanity, Dishonesty, Suspicion, Jealousy, Cowardice, Knavery, Reserve, Ignorance, Bassess d'Esprit & I know not what, to every thing opposite to it, busy Industry, Frankness, Neatness, well loaded Tables plain good manners, an obliging attention Firmness, Intelligence, &, thank God, Cheerfulness, & above [all], Honesty, which I solemnly swear I have not looked full in the Face since I first passed to the Eastward & Northward of the Baltic. Once more welcome Europe to my warmest Embraces. . . .

Let no European put entire Confidence in a Russian of whatever Condition and none at all in the lower & middle Ranks of People.

3 THE NATIONAL CHARACTER IS FAR FROM BEING SAVAGE

New-York Magazine

The *New-York Magazine* was one of the four most important American periodicals of the late eighteenth century. Travel reports occupied a considerable place in its files. A large part of its material was taken from books and other magazines and published without reference to its origin—as may have been the article of May, 1792, from which the following excerpts have been taken.[76]

The article distinguishes clearly between the adverse effects of the oppressive social and political conditions on the mental and spiritual life of the people, and their national character traits. The latter are seen in a favorable light, although—in typical eighteenth-century fashion—the manifestations of these traits are deplored as the result of uncontrolled and undirected emotions and not of sane reasoning and steady and firm principles.

RUSSIA IS ALMOST the only country in Europe in which the people do not enjoy a show of civil privilege, or some kind of semblance of political right. The Souvereign is not only despotic, but every individual subject a slave. The first Noble of the land is the immediate slave of the Crown, and the wealth of every man in Russia solely consists in the number of slaves which he himself possesses. Thus the lower orders of the Community are in the most abject state of being to which human nature can be reduced.—They are the slaves of slaves, perhaps through several degradations.

A Russian peasant has no property, his miserable earnings, his offspring, and almost his life, are at the capricious disposal of his master. Divested of property, exposed to unmerited cruelty and insult, and sinking under oppression, he looks not beyond the gloomy period of the passing hour. Indolence and inertion are the consequences, and he scarcely soars in mental endowment above the humiliating level of the irrational creation. The hereditary victim of avarice and oppression, he has no inducement to labour but the dread of punishment, and thus exposed to the unabating rigour of some petty tyrant, his mind becomes hardened and inhuman.

The national character of the Russians as it has been presented by the most accurate and philosophic observers, is far from being savage or even unamiable. They possess strong sensibility, from whence flow the brightest effusions that decorate the human mind, but it is unhappily in them wholly unsubdued and undirected by reason. Hence they are betrayed, not only into inconsistencies, but often into crimes. Their feelings are ever in extremes. The most trivial enjoyments elevate them to the summit of happiness, the slightest disappointments plunge them to the lowest depths of despair. Those of irregular sensibility in any Country, are courageous or cowardly, according to the impulse of the moment, unless their sensibility be chastised and regulated by the calm suggestions of reason. Steady and unmoveable resolution is founded alone upon fixed and undeviating principles. Mere animal courage is subject to all the varieties of our feeble nature. Hence the Russians, acting upon no specific and permanent principle, are brave or dastardly, as the feelings of the moment inspire. Reflection never comes in aid of nature, and at times even a distant and trivial danger appalls him, while on other occasions he will act as if he were incapable of apprehension, constitutionally destitute of every sense of danger. In the armies of Russia, the latter sometimes produces the most brilliant effects; while the former is guarded against and corrected by the strictest military discipline. . . .

The Russian soldier unites not with military service its brightest ornament, *the feelings and the sentiments of a free and enlightened* CITIZEN: of the justice of the cause in which he is engaged, he is incompetent to judge—for neither the principles or the practice of moral justice has ever been made obvious to his dulled and violated senses, and he moves a devoted victim at the shrine of lawless ambition and unsatiable power.

4 A PERSONABLE PEOPLE, HARDY AND VIGOROUS

Jedidiah Morse (1761–1826)

Originally a clergyman, Jedidiah Morse shifted his interests to geography. His publications in this field earned him the name of Father of American Geography. He had never traveled to Russia and his knowledge of the country was, therefore, secondhand. Essentially a compiler, he drew on available American and European sources as well as on information that reached him in letters and other materials from all parts of the country in response to his published requests.

The picture of the Russians drawn in his *American Universal Geography* of 1793, our next selection,[77] is not unflattering. He credits them with physical strength, hardiness, and endurance. According to him they have not yet fully emerged from their semi-barbarous state, but amenities of life have progressed to the point where "a French or English gentleman may now live as comfortably in Russia as in other parts of Europe." The thought that an American might also consider living in Russia was not entertained by Morse. During the early years of their country, few Americans may have had the leisure for a trip to Russia or the inclination to take residence in that country.

•————————————————————————————————•

THE RUSSIANS, properly so called, are in general a personable people, hardy, vigorous, and patient of labour, especially in the field, to an incredible degree. Their complexions differ little from those of the

English or Scots; but their women think that an addition of red heightens their beauty. Their eye-sight seems to be defective, occasioned, probably, by the snow, which for a long time of the year is continually present to their eyes. Their officers and soldiers always possessed a large share of passive valour; but in the late war with the king of Prussia [1757–1761], they proved as active as any troops in Europe; and in the late war with the Turks [1787–1791] they greatly distinguished themselves. They are implicitly submissive to discipline, let it be ever so severe; they endure extreme hardships with great patience; and can content themselves with very hard fare.

Before the days of Peter the Great [1682–1725], the Russians were in general barbarous, ignorant, mean, and much addicted to drunkenness; no less than 4000 brandy shops have been reckoned in Moskow. Not only the common people but many of the boyards or nobles, lived in a continual state of idleness and intoxication; and the most complete objects of misery and barbarity presented themselves upon the streets, while the court of Moskow was by far the most splendid of any upon the globe. The czar and the grandees dressed after the most superb Asiatic manner; and their magnificence exceeded every idea that can be conceived from modern examples. The Earl of Carlisle in the account of his embassy, says, that he could see nothing but gold and precious stones in the robes of the czar and his courtiers. The manufactures, however, of these and all other luxuries, were carried on by Italians, Germans, and other foreigners. Peter saw the bulk of his subjects, at his accession to the throne, little better than beasts of burden to support the pomp of the court. He forced his great men to lay aside their long robes and dress in the European manner; and he even obliged the laity to cut off their beards. The Russians, before his days, had hardly a ship upon their coasts. They had no conveniences for travelling, no pavements in their streets, no places of public diversion; and they entertained a souvereign contempt for all improvements of the mind. At present, a French or English gentleman may live as comfortably and sociably in Russia, as in most other parts of Europe. Their polite assemblies, since the accession of the present empress, have been put under proper regulations; and few of the ancient usages remain. It is, however, said that they are yet addicted to intemperance.

The Russians were formerly noted for so strong an attachment to their native soil, that they seldom visited foreign parts. The Russian nobility, however, besides those who are in a publick character, are now found at every court in Europe. Her imperial majesty [Catherine II, the Great] even interests herself in the education of young men of quality in the knowledge of the world, and foreign services.

It is said that the Russian ladies were formerly as submissive to their husbands in their families, as the latter are to their superiors in the field; and that they thought themselves ill-treated if they were not often reminded of their duty by the discipline of a whip, manufactured by themselves, which they presented to their husbands on the day of their marriage. Their nuptial ceremonies are peculiar to themselves; and formerly consisted of some whimsical rites, many of which are now disused. When the parents are agreed upon a match, though the parties have never seen each other, the bride is examined stark naked by a certain number of females, who are to correct, if possible, any defects they find in her person. On her wedding day she is crowned with a garland of wormwood, and after the priest has tied the nuptial knot, his clerk or sexton throws a handful of hops upon the head of the bride, wishing that she may prove as fruitful as that plant. She is then led home, with abundance of coarse, and indeed indecent ceremonies, which are now wearing off even among the lowest ranks; and the barbarous treatment of wives by their husbands, which extended even to scouring or broiling them to death, is either guarded against by the laws of the country, or by particular stipulations in the marriage contract. . . .

The Russians are remarkable for the severity, barbarity and variety of their punishments, which are both inflicted and endured with a wonderful insensibility. . . . according to the strict letter of the law, there are no capital punishments in Russia, except in the case of high treason. But when this matter is thoroughly investigated, there is much less humanity in it than has been supposed. For there are many felons who die under the knout, and others die of fatigue in their journeys to Siberia, and from the hardships they suffer in the mines; so that there is reason to believe, that no fewer criminals suffer death in Russia than in those countries wherein capital punishments are authorized by the laws.

A RUSSIAN PRIEST

A COSSACK GUARD

MAIL-DRIVER AND GUARD

ON THE MARCH TO SIBERIA

AN EXILE SETTLEMENT

5 WE MUST LOOK AMONG THE PEASANTS FOR THE TRUE NATIONAL CHARACTER

Literary Museum, West-Chester, Pa.

In February 1797 the following essay, "Manners and Customs of the Russian Peasants," was sent anonymously to the *Literary Museum*,[78] a magazine that had recently made its appearance. The author signed his letter of transmittal as "Historicus." While largely a factual report, it contains references to the characteristics of the peasantry, the great majority of the Russian people. They are described as hardly industrious, though not averse to working when they must. On the whole they are portrayed as yet in a primitive state, ignorant, and superstitious, but at the same time as very human, essentially honest, personally clean, friendly, and very hospitable.

THE RUSSIAN GENTLEMEN have almost adopted the same manner of living as that of the other nations of Europe. The citizens being for the most part, slaves who have been made free, retain, in a great measure, the manners of their primitive state, and are very few in number. It is amongst the peasants, therefore that we must look for the true national character of the Russians. Some of them are slaves of the crown, and the rest, who form the great number, are slaves to the great lords, who have every power over them, except that of life and death. The Russian peasants were originally free; but about the middle of the sixteenth century, they were made part of every estate, in order to prevent emigration. Since that period a custom has prevailed of treating them entirely as serfs, or selling and buying them, and of transferring them as property in any other manner. Their yoke, however, is much easier than that of the peasants of Livonia, because the Livonian gentlemen consider theirs as procured by conquest, while the Russian peasants have the same origin as their masters.

The ordinary food of the Russian peasants, besides bread is the *schutschi*, that is to say a kind of a soup made of cabbage, rendered sour by fermentation, and hashed very small: this soup is for the most part accompanied by a piece of boiled meat. Their drink is *kivas*; a sort of sour yellowish small beer which they brew themselves in large earthen pans. Their dress consists of a shirt always very neat, which hangs over their breeches, a linen frock, a surtout shaped like their frock, and made of coarse woollen cloth; the whole descends as low as their knees, and is fastened to the body with a girdle. In winter instead of a surtout, they wear a cloak of sheep skin, their heads are bare in summer, and in winter covered with a cap.

They wear no covering to their necks either winter or summer; their legs are wrapt up in bandages of cloth; but they use shoes, or rather a kind of slippers made of the rind of trees cut into slips, which are interwoven together. The women are dressed almost in the same manner as the men; but their exterior garments are loose, and not fastened with a girdle; they are also very long, and reach down to their feet.

Their wooden huts have all a resemblance one to another. They are built in villages, bordering the highway, are placed parallel to it, and are covered with boards. Nothing is seen but a wall formed of planks, having two or three holes in it, which serve as windows. These windows are only large enough for one to put the head through them. They are seldom filled with squares of glass; but in the inside there is a piece of wood to shut them during the night, or in the time of bad weather. On the one side of the hut is a small gate, which conducts to the yard, the greater part of which is covered with wooden planks to shelter their carts, hay, &c. From the yard you enter the house by a back door, to which you go up by a few steps, and when you have opened the door, you find in the first corner, towards the right hand, a stove constructed of bricks, which serves them for culinary purposes, and to warm the apartment. Around the stove, and on a level with its top, runs a circular projection upon which the family sleep and take a forenoon nap, as well as on the stove itself, however warm it may be; for they are remarkably fond of excessive heat; and in the corner opposite the stove, in a diagonal direction, that is to say, in the corner on the left, stands a small wooden shelf, at about the height of a man containing a few images of their saints, ranged in order, and surrounded by small wax candles or lamps which are lighted on certain festivals; the drapery of these saints is embossed, and formed of tin plate or of copper, gilt; but the visage, the hands, the feet, and in general all the naked parts, are only painted. The Russians pretend that they are authorized to have painted images, but none of carved work, because the commandment says, "Thou shalt not make unto thee any graven image." All around the hut is a wooden bench, made for sitting or sleeping upon. Nearer the door than the saints, and to the left as you enter, is a long table, formed of two boards, joint together lengthwise and before it, on one side the bench already mentioned, and on the other side a portable-bench much narrower. The rest of the furniture consists of a wooden bason, suspended from the roof, on one side of the stove, in order to wash their hands whenever cleanliness requires it; a wooden platter, two or three wooden dishes, and a few wooden spoons.

As the hut forms only one apartment, all mix together without any distinction; one may see sleeping on the earth, on the bench, or on the top of the stove, the master of the house, the mistress, the children, and servants, both male and female, and all without any scandal. In some huts, however, there is a particular corner for the master and mistress, but it is separated from the rest only by a curtain, suspended from a pole placed in a horizontal direction. These huts have no chimneys; the smoke, therefore, renders them exceedingly black in the inside. If they are entered at the time when the mistress of the family is preparing dinner, the smoke, and the smell of the onions, which they use in all their dishes, do not fail to make those sick who are not accustomed to them. When the smoke becomes too powerful to be resisted they open a small wicket, which is a little higher window, in order to give it vent; but the peasants do this with reluctance, as they fear that part of the heat may escape at the same time; they are fond of being as it were roasted in their huts.

These peasants supply all their wants; they make their own shoes, benches, tables, wooden dishes, and construct their own stoves, and huts. The females also weave a kind of cloth which resembles a very broad ribband; they have occasion, therefore, to buy only a little woollen cloth or sheep-skins to cover them; their girdles, which they consider as objects of great luxury, and the iron they employ for their implements of husbandry.

The Russian peasants are temperate in eating but not in drinking; they are extremely fond of strong liquors, and often get intoxicated, especially on their festivals. They think they would not show their respect for their saints, did they not honor them by getting drunk; and they have a word to express the state in which one finds one's self next day. They call this state, between health and sickness, *spoklimelie*; the women are addicted to drinking as well as men. They cannot be accused of lazyness; but they consider labor as necessary evil, and never execute any piece of work thoroughly, contenting themselves with finishing it in a very imperfect manner; for this reason therefore, they scratch up the ground, instead of tilling it. They are fond of keeping their persons neat; however dirty their upper garments may be, their shirts are always clean; they have warm or evaporated baths, into which the men and women, boys and girls, without distinction, plunge themselves two or three times a week. An order has lately been made, forbidding different sexes to mix together promiscuously in these baths; but this order is very little observed.

They marry when very young, and often even at the command of their masters. Paternal authority among them is very great, and it continues during the lives of their children; a father may give a blow with a stick to his son of whatever age or condition he may be. We are told, that an old peasant having gone to visit his son, who had made a fortune in the army, and who enjoyed a considerable rank, the latter was so proud of his promotion, that he ordered his domesticks to send the old man about his business. The father, how-ever having found means to enter the house when none of the servants were in the way, took a large cudgel, and gave his son a sound beating; nor did the son, so powerful was presented authority, dare to defend himself, or to call out for assistance.

The people in Russia are very hospitable. A Russian peasant, when on a journey, enters whatever house he chooses, makes the sign of the cross before an image, salutes the company, and lays down his knapsack without any ceremony. If he finds the family at table, he says *bread and salt*, upon which the master of the house replies, *eat my bread*, and the stranger immediately places himself among the company. If he happens to arrive when the people are not at meals, he sits down among the rest without any formality at the proper time. If it be in the evening, he sleeps in the hut, and the next morning departs very early without saying a word: if the family are up, he says, I thank you for bread and salt. A stranger who is travelling, meets with almost the same hospitality, if he can be satisfied with the usual fare of these peasants; if he cannot, he must pay the full price for every thing extraordinary; he pays also for the hay which the horses have eat; but the price is always moderate.

Whatever little money these peasants acquire, they place it behind their images, and commit it to their care. Robbery is never heard among them, although the doors of their huts are always open, and often left without any person to guard them. However disinterested the Russians may be naturally, they soon become fond of money, especially when they begin to trade; they have then a perfect resemblance to the Jews; they are as exorbitant in the prices which they ask, and equally ready to take every advantage, but at the same time they are equally disposed to sell with a small profit, when they cannot get rid of their goods in any other manner.

These peasants are not sullen, like those of Germany; they speak much, are very polite, and even sometimes to excess. Their mode of saluting is by shaking one another by the hand, and by bowing. Their equals they call brothers, and their superiors they call fathers. Before their lords, and before those from whom they ask a favour, they prostrate themselves, that is to say, stretch themselves out at their length on the ground. These Russians have very little ambition. If you speak to them with mildness, you may obtain from them whatever you desire; and they will not be offended when you call them knaves and cheats and even much worse. They are very honest; but when they cease to be so, one cannot use too much precaution not to be a dupe to their promises. Their minds receive very little cultivation, for they can neither read nor write; all their learning consists in a few proverbs, which they transmit from father to son. They are fond of vocal musick, and are always singing. The labourer sings behind the plow, the coachman on his box, and the carpenter on the roof of the hut where he is at work; their songs are generally upon love, and their musick is very monotonous.

The religion of the Russians is that of the Greek church; that of these peasants consists in going to hear mass, in prostrating themselves evening and morning before their images, saying *ghospodi pomiloni*, Lord have pity upon me! in making the sign of the cross before and after meals, or when passing a church, and lastly in observing Lent.

The last article is absolutely indispensible [sic]; a Russian peasant is firmly persuaded that God would sooner pardon murder than a violation of Lent. Their priests are equally ignorant as themselves; all their learning consists in knowing their ritual pretty well, and in being able to give a benediction, even in the streets to those who ask it, gratis, or for the value of a penny, or a halfpenny.

6 FALSE CONCEPTIONS OF MAGNIFICENCE AND EMPIRE

Literary Magazine, Philadelphia

The *Literary Magazine* was founded in 1803 by Charles Brockden Brown and continued publication until 1810. It gave special attention to political reports and general news.

In 1806 Russia was a member of the coalition against Napoleon. Americans who looked at the European scene wondered about the role that that empire would play in the battles against Napoleon. Apparently, American opinions on Russian political and military strength were uncertain and vacillating. This was reflected in the pages of the *Literary Magazine*. Issues prior to the one of December, 1806, from which the following unsigned article[79] has been excerpted, had spoken of Russia's advances in arts and sciences, in commerce and politics. While the distance between the "ignorance and poverty of Russia" and the civilized world of Western Europe was seen as great, Russia was considered to have made rapid progress "in civilization and refinement."

•————————————————————————————•

RUSSIA, BY THE PART she has recently taken in the contests and negotiations of the western nations of Europe, has become an object of importance. The progress and condition, political and geographical, of that empire, are subjects of curious speculation; but these speculations seem hitherto to have led to many erroneous conclusions. It is common to allow our minds to be overwhelmed by the magnitude of this object and not to discriminate between the real and apparent sources of power and wealth.

From surveys . . . we are apt to obtain awful conceptions of the greatness of Russia. When we compare it with the western parts of Europe, and observe that England and Wales, multiplied eighty fold, would be no more than equal in extent to Russia; that France, Spain, or Germany is to this empire as one is to twenty-five; the former kingdoms are likely to fall into contempt, to dwindle into insignificance.

These lofty images, however, will perhaps be somewhat lowered when we come to reflect that ground, not inhabited or cultivated, and not capable of cultivation, is in reality of no more value, in an estimate of national greatness, than so much water. A million acres of sand, or bog, or *glaciers*, is, indeed inferior to a million acres of ocean: since the water abounds with life and motion, and supplies an inexhaustible store of subsistence to those who seek it; but the snows and fogs of Kamchatka, the dreary sands of Orenburg and Tobolsk, and the mountainous rocks of Yakutska, afford no scope for the plough, no nutrition to the wholesome plants on which civilized man must live, and no air fit to be inhaled by human lungs.

In estimating national power, one consideration is the number of subjects. Three-fourths of this empire are comprised in Siberia; but Siberia is a realm of torpor, solitude, and dreariness. One-fifth of it lies within the arctic circle and is wandered over by a few thousands of human creatures, whose animal and mental powers are withered and shrunk up by the horrors of the climate. . . .

What is pompously called the Russian empire in Asia, is a nominal and unsettled superiority over savage tribes and barren deserts. Its subjects are poor and barbarous, and dispersed, in small bands, hundreds of miles from each other; and with few exceptions, vagabonds and rovers, without a fixed dwelling or a tilled acre. . . .

European Russia is a country of immense extent . . . It will be nearer, and certainly not fall below the truth, to fix the number of European Russian subjects at *twenty millions*: but this does not exceed the population of France or Germany, and how immeasurable is the interval between the ignorance and poverty of Russia, and the arts and opulence of Flanders or Saxony!

In no country in the world are the false conceptions of magnificence and empire more prevalent than in Russia; no where have the efforts to enlarge dominion been more uniform and strenuous; no where has the art of transforming men into soldiers been practised to a greater extent. Yet the utmost military force which these vast territories can furnish, including the licentious bands of Tartar cavalry, have never exceeded the regular force of France or Austria.

In estimating national power, the importance of numbers is lessened in proportion as they are scattered over a wider space, as they are poor, ignorant, disunited, and imperfectly subjected. In all these respects, Russia may be quoted as a perfect specimen of political debility. There is no region of the globe, in which numbers have a less proportion to extent of ground, whose soil is more sterile, and climate more unfriendly to man; whose inhabitants are more ferocious and stupid, and forlorn, and more remote from each other in language, habits, and religion; and where the rights of souvereignty are less perfectly established, less profitable to the rulers, and less beneficial to the subjects.

As Russia extends in civilization and refinement, her wants will increase and her commerce extend; the soil and climate around this [Baltic] sea will derive every assistance from so great a power, and the encouragement given to commercial adventure in general, which is so much fostered as it is, by his present imperial majesty, that it may probably soon become very great, and be the cause of giving an entire new turn, not only to the commerce of the Baltic, but most likely, to the politics of Europe.

7 EUROPEAN STANDARDS DO NOT APPLY

Robert Walsh, Jr. (1784–1859)

Robert Walsh, Jr., a writer and journalist, devoted considerable attention to European affairs throughout his life. After reading law, he traveled and studied in France and England. Returning to the United States, he settled in Philadelphia. He became known as the editor of the *American Register* and the founder of the *American Review of History and Politics*, as well as the author of an *Essay on the Future State of Europe*. With his former law teacher, Robert Godloe Harper, he had an exchange of correspondence on European affairs, which was published in 1813 under the title *Correspondence Respecting Russia*. Excerpts from that book follow as the next selection.[80] The correspondence dealt with the effect on the European balance of power of Napoleon's defeat in his campaign against Russia in 1812. Walsh had little disagreement with Harper on essentials. The argument concerned mainly the question of whether or not Napoleon was finished.

Walsh's disapproving comments on serfdom in Russia, which appear at the end of the selection, seem to be in consonance with his views on slavery in the United States. He had been the founder of the *National Gazette* of Philadelphia and was connected with that paper for fifteen years while it was known for its unpopular views favoring abolition.

● ─────────────────────────────── ●

THERE IS NO GOVERNMENT, or people, on record, whose history is more atrocious, in almost every stage. It is, particularly until the commencement of the last century, one shocking tissue of cruelty, perfidy, ruthless vengeance, and insatiable ambition:—The people brutal, ferocious, and slavish, to the last degree; the government fitted in every respect to foster their vices; wildly sanguinary and anarchical within; not less arbitrary than mutable, both at home and abroad; always prone to plunder and oppress. Such rulers as Peter and Catherine, and Alexander, anomalies in the system, serve to exhibit both government and people, under a better and delusive aspect. Without doubt these monarchs have not laboured in vain for the improvement of their subjects. Much more has been accomplished by them, than the nature of the case seems to admit: But the fundamental character remains.

I know, indeed, that the modern refined theory, or even the motley practice, of civilized Europe, is not the standard by which we can fairly estimate the Russians, either as to their early history, whether domestic or foreign, or their conduct at any period, toward those savage neighbors and rivals, with whom they waged unavoidable wars of intercession. These wars, on which their national importance, not to say existence, continued to be staked, to the middle of the last century, and in which they were unremittingly engaged with extreme vicissitudes of fortune; their prostration for a long term under the horrible Tartar yoke; their sanguinary and almost continual intestine commotions; the grim and stupifying despotism of their own formation; the peculiar inveteracy of the oriental barbarism with which they were deeply infected, far more gross and intractable than the Gothic;—naturally retarded their progress in civilization, and maintained them, until recently, in a state analogous to that, in which the southern and western nations of Europe are represented to have been, in the early ages.

In pronouncing sentence on the Russians, we should take, for equity's sake, as the measure of their demerit, and our reprobation, the genius, morals and habits of our own Saxon and Vandal progenitors, and not those of the Britain of the present day, or the Gaul of the eighteenth century. Revolutionary and Imperial Gaul, indeed, is a test to be avoided with equal care, lest we should be betrayed into the opposite extreme,—of undue admiration, and fall, with respect to the Muscovites, under an error like that which Rousseau laboured to propagate, in relation to savage man in general. . . .

The civilization of an immense people composed of seventy or eighty different nations, contaminated with oriental barbarism, scattered over a vast extent of country, cannot be the work of a moment —can be effected only by slow and almost imperceptible degrees. There is a material difference between civilizing a great empire or only a few districts, or a few individuals. A rude nation, it has been justly remarked, may appear to have made much progress, when compared only with herself, as to what she originally was, but scarcely better than stationary, when exhibited by the side of countries truly refined. I need not suggest to you, how much the designs of the most active and benevolent prince must be impeded, and the general reformation delayed, by such a constitution both political and civil as that of Russia; without any formal check to the executive power; without a dignified magistracy, or a regular body of legal professors; not only with the leprosy of bondage tainting and palsying the mass, but the most odious and depressing distinctions estranging those who are free.

The agriculture of Russia although exuberantly productive on account of the general fertility of the soil, is acknowledged by all travellers to be extremely unskilful and imperfect. Being left almost entirely to the serfs not merely as labourers but farmers, it cannot be otherwise. A merely natural and artless husbandry such as they practice with the most clumsy utensils, does little towards the improvement of the mind or style of being, and not much towards population. Great natural advantages, and the development of her commerce, may have induced in Russia even a considerable increase of numbers, and some amelioration in the rural economy of the southern and western districts of her European empire, together with a certain progress in the useful arts; without leading, however, to a correspondent advancement in the feelings and reasonings and manners of civilization. These may have been checked by certain inveterate prejudices and habits of barbarism, superstition, and slavery.

I have been told that this idea is verified, more particularly in her easterly provinces even of Europe. The same gross modes of exist- ence, the same extravagancies of fanaticism, the same proclivity to servitude, the same abjectness of soul, the same tinct of insubordination, continue to prevail as formerly, with modifications and exceptions indeed, but these hardly of sufficient consequence to be taken into the account. How can the case be other, where domestic slavery still obtains to such an extent, under its most hideous aspect, and with most of its worst attributes?

LIVING-ROOM OF RUSSIAN PEASANT'S HOUSE AT UST KARÁ

8 A DISTANT AND DAZZLING PROSPECT

David Ramsay (1749–1815)

A versatile and gifted man, David Ramsay is best remembered as a historian of the American Revolution and of the first decades of the United States. He had started out as a physician, but had left medicine to enter politics. He was a delegate to the Continental Congress and eventually served in the House and the Senate. Various business ventures that he undertook were less successful than his contributions to medicine, politics, and history. His *Universal History Americanised*, from which the following selection has been taken,[81] was published posthumously in 1819.

Ramsay's remarks on Russia show that he wrote the *Universal History Americanised* when Russian fortunes in Europe were reaching their zenith, after Napoleon's retreat from Moscow in the winter of 1812. His strong bias in favor of Protestantism betrays his partisanship for England, then an enemy of Roman Catholic France.

•——————————————————————•

RUSSIA IS BUT LITTLE ADVANCED in evangelical knowledge or practice, yet it may justly be regarded as a favourable circumstance, that its growing intercourse with the more polished nations of Europe naturally leads to a higher state of civilization, and to a more extensive cultivation of literature. And as the most intimate connections of Russia are with those protestant nations in which the power of godliness most prevails, it cannot but afford many and great opportunities for the admission of truth and godliness, among them, especially as the policy of the government holds out encouragement to the settlement of foreigners, and indulges all protestants with

61

toleration. This has already produced some happy effects in the little colony of Germans on the Wolga. It is a great advantage that Christianity is the general profession, that the orthodox creeds are professed by the national belief, and, however low the present state of spiritual religion may be among them, a door of hope is open for the admission of farther light and truth. . . .

With so vast a population, so formidable a military force, so ample a revenue, and such immense resources of every kind, it is no wonder that her influence should be predominant in Europe and Asia. She alone, among the continental powers, has nothing to fear from the exorbitant aggrandizement of France.

The numerous population of Russia, diffused over so vast an extent of country, and comprehending a number of barbarous tribes, is a less effective support of military enterprise than a concentrated mass of people, crowded within narrow territory; forming its levies with greater rapidity; and directing more expeditiously, its force toward any requisite point. Such are the comparative circumstances of Russia and France. The European part of the empire, indeed, contains the principal mass of Russian population, which is supposed to be not less than 32,000,000. Russia has much more to gain in the east than in the west of Europe; and the Ottoman Porte has everything to apprehend from her continually increasing power. The Christians of Greece, Asia Minor, and Syria, are secretly attached to Russia and certain combinations of political circumstances may produce, in that quarter, great and sudden revolutions. If we extend our views into futurity, and imagine a period when Russia shall attain to that complete population which she is endeavoring, by a multiplicity of means, to acquire, and to which, according to the most authentic documents, and the evidence of visible circumstances, she is continually approximating, in an ascending ratio, this immense empire presents a distant and dazzling prospect which opens a wide field, both for political and moral speculation. Such a period, whenever it shall arrive, whether we suppose the continued union, or the division of the empire, cannot but be productive of extraordinary revolutions, both in Europe and in Asia. Russia, in a united state, with a compact population, must sway the destinies of these two quarters of the globe. . . .

The literature of Russia is yet in its infancy. The inhabitants of those countries, which had once been under the dominion of the Romans, had imbibed the learning and arts of that people; and, amidst the darkness of the Gothic ages, some remnants were preserved among the monastic orders. But Russia was destitute of this advantage. At the time of Vladimir's conversion [988 or 989], the empire had not emerged from barbarism. Literature, as in other countries, immediately succeeded the introduction of Christianity; but its transient light was soon extinguished amidst the scenes of internal division, and of Tartarian oppression, which afterwards followed. The modern literature of Russia must be considered as the work of the last century; and especially of the reign of the last empress. Like other nations, indeed, Russia has long had her fabricators of legends, her compilers of martyrologies, and a few writers of annals. But Russian literature was a barren subject till the auspicious reign of Catherine, who, by her example and patronage, greatly encouraged its cultivation. Even during that period, most of the principal writers . . . were foreigners, and used the German language, so that the sphere of Russian literature is yet very contracted, although all possible means have lately been employed to promote its extension. Russian authors have appeared, whose works have acquired a deserved celebrity, and exhibit sufficient proofs of the national genius. Illustrious names might be added in various departments of literary composition, which, like every thing in Russia, is in a state of progressive advancement. Periodical publications, however, have hitherto met with little success.

The polite arts, as well as science and letters, are yet in their infant state. Most of the eminent artists are foreigners, but Russia can boast of a few native names. The various institutions for the advancement of arts, sciences, and literature, both in the residence of the court, and in the ancient capital, have already been mentioned in general terms. . . . The general sketch, here presented, is perhaps sufficient to shew that no nation, of the ancient world, has surpassed Russia in the greatness of its recent efforts for improvement, and none, in the modern, has equalled it, except the United States of America.

9 THIS NATION IS FAR BEHIND ALL OTHERS IN EUROPE

William David Lewis (1792–1881)

After an apprenticeship in business, William David Lewis joined his older brother, a merchant in St. Petersburg, in 1814. He remained there for ten years, one of nine or ten Americans living in Russia. When he had a fight with his uncle Leavitt Harris, the United States consul, he was imprisoned by Russian authorities. The quarrel was continued in the United States, where the two fought a duel. To gather evidence for a resulting lawsuit, Lewis made another trip to Russia.

Obviously a spirited fellow, Lewis made broad contacts in Russian political and literary circles, having devoted himself to the study of the language upon his first arrival. Although in later life he became a successful financier and banker in the United States, he remained interested in Russia and Russian literature and published translations of Russian poetry.

The following letter, written to Edward Coles, President Madison's personal envoy to Russia, contains observations of a general nature. Its moralistic and sanctimonious tone may reflect the polite respect with which Lewis addressed himself to a personage representing the president. But it also mirrors the reactions of "a young American of that day living in a cultural milieu markedly different from what he experienced in the United States."[82]

St. Petersburg. October 7th, 1816

E. Coles Esqr.

Dear Sir:

Herewith I hand you the observations on the Customs and of the Russians, which I promised you the other day: their only Recommendation is their truth. I have sent Copies of them to several of my friends in America, you must not therefore be surprised if you should ever meet with them in other hands.

Observations.

The Peasants of Russia are in a state of slavery much the same as the Blacks in the southern parts of America, though held by individuals in infinitely greater numbers. There are some noblemen who own 20, 30, 40, 50, and one or two even as many as 100, thousand Males. These poor people are obliged to work their Masters' lands and pay them a Tax amounting annually to from 20 to 30 Rubles per soul; from this tax the women are exempted, though not from the share of labour. The Peasants generally work as much land for themselves as their Lord, it being understood that half their time belongs to themselves; it is by the product of this portion of their time that they are enabled to raise the tax in money, besides which their Masters never refuse them the privilege of leaving their Estates in the winter to go in search of Employment, a sufficient number remaining at home to do the little that is to be done there in that dreary and inactive season. Their employment mostly consists in transporting Merchandize from City to City, or in performing in the towns the duties of *Izvoshtshicks* or Drivers, each Peasant who can afford it generally taking with him a little sledge (called in America Sled, which word is hooted at by the *learned Europeans*!) and horse: at that season there are so many of them in the streets that a person may ride about for the merest trifle.

The Condition of a Russian Peasant is by no means so miserable as would appear at first sight: their houses are of log substantially & comfortably built, and they always live together in villages some of which are very large; the gable ends of their houses universally front the street, which renders them, it is said, much warmer than if built in the mode practiced by us, a less portion of them being exposed to the weather, for they with their appendages, say [i.e.] low houses, extend a considerable distance back, and usually stand together very compactly. The general food of the Peasantry is simple to be sure, but they have enough of it, and are not less healthy than those who feast on delicacies. It consists of very black Ryebread (This is the favorite Bread of the nobility also, though both wheat and Rye are mostly met with at their tables.) and salt, the bread being sour, but not ill flavored. Carrots, Turnips, Parsnips, Beans, Peas, Onions, and most other vegetables they eat raw; their drink is an acid and to me most nauseous liquor made of grain (mostly of rye or barley) and called Quass, or more properly Kvass, but it is healthy and drunk by the Russians of all classes & both sexes in no small quantities. They have a Brandy, too, distilled from Grain, which the lower orders drink to great excess, being almost universally drunkards. They are goodnatured however, and may in a general way be bribed to do anything, but they are naturally very knavish and tricky. Their state is about demi-barbarous, yet they possess a wonderful degree of innate politeness and grace, so that the lowest boor will talk to his master with all the ease and fluency of an equal, never however forgetting for a moment his respect and obedience. Their eloquence is proverbial among the foreigners resident here and the grammatical propriety with which they speak their native language is a subject of wonder to all who are acquainted with it, even to the higher classes of their own countrymen. Their dress consists of a long woolen Coat called in Russian Kaftan, reaching nearly down to their heels and covering their pantaloons entirely; this they tie around their waists with a worsted sash; their hats are broad brimmed and bell-crowned, but in winter they mostly wear Caps lined with some cheap fur; the better kind of them have leather boots, but a vast number of them wear basketwrought shoes of birch bark, and wrap rags around their legs to serve instead of stockings. The Kaftan properly speaking is worn only *in common* by the richer Peasants, or put on as a Dress, the usual garb in the villages being a sheep skin made up in the shape of the Kaftan, which they call a shoob or *tvoloos*, and which they wear alike the hottest day in summer and the coldest in winter. The Russians in general (i.e., the lower classes still, say Peasants and Merchants) wear their beards long from a religious superstition; this they adhere to strictly, and if they are asked the reason their answer is, "God commands us."

The Women of the Country are generally ugly, particularly among the Peasantry, who are extremely dirty and slovenly about their persons. Their features bear throughout a striking resemblance, being of the Tartar cast. Almost all the Russian women have little sunken eyes, pug noses, and high cheekbones, faces devoid of expression, or if professing any, it being rather of the disagreeable kind. In going Southwesterly however, their features improve, in Mosco many of Merchants' Daughters are quite handsome, and in Toola and Catorga [*sic*] comeliness is more frequently met with than in Mosco: St. Petersburg has less claim as to the beauty of its women than any town I have yet seen either in Russia or elsewhere. The married Ladies among the Nobility are very familiar, and easy in their manners, but the Merchants, being universally of low extraction and badly educated, keep their wives and daughters under as much restraints as the husbands and fathers of eastern countries. The daughter of a Russian Merchant being consequently altogether unaccustomed to the company or conversation of young men, feels excessively awkward and confused if by any chance she finds herself in their society, and is sure to get out of it as fast as she can. In Mosco, where everything is more national than in St. Petersburg, on their meeting a stranger, being ashamed to look him in the face, they make a low inclination of the head, so that I felt not a little pleased on my arrival there, to find myself so often saluted with such respect by fair creatures whom I had never before seen in my life. I returned however their *Zdrastvouitee* (how d'ye do?) with the best air I could, hoping by that means to get into their good graces and fancying that a thousand happy adventures and fortunate intrigues must be the inevitable result of such a kind and flattering predeliction as they all appeared to express in my favor!

"Vain hopes oft youthful fancies blind
and make a *nincom.* of the mind.
By visions fair and pictures gay
The happy youth they lead astray.
With bright ideas his head they fill
And give him pleasure's cup to swill.
Yet ever whilst with raptured brain
Anxious the honied dream to train,
Ere he in guzzling of the draught
Has one good swallow fairly, quaff'd.
Fortune gives the goblet a tilt
And all the precious juice is spilt!"
—The Journey, on a Tour in the South

The ladies have a most unaccountable practice of rubbing their teeth with some vile composition which takes off the enamel and makes them black as coal; this is considered by many of them as a beauty, so that I have sometimes seen girls of 16 or 17, of no common comliness for this northern region, display on opening their lips a row of teeth so black and hideous as to shock me. The custom of blackening their teeth thus some Travellers have represented as universal among the women of this Country, this like many others of their assertions is untrue; the most that can be said of it is that it is not very uncommon, it is not however by any means general. The strict manner in which this class of women is brought up may be imagined when I state that a particular friend of mine, a German Gentleman of undoubted veracity, who had lived a long time in Mosco, assured me that in one instance he had been very intimate in the house of a Russian Merchant for several years and never knew he had a daughter till he at length espied her one day by accident, peeping at him through the crevice of the door. The young lady at that time was nearly full grown.

The Nobility for the most part speak French, but the Merchants very rarely any language but their own & even *that*, few among them are capable of writing correctly; this arises from the circum- stance of the orthography being extremely difficult on account of the great approximation of several letters to each other in sound, so that good orthography in Russian can only be expected of persons educated better than is customary. The liberty allowed to unmarried ladies of all classes is far less than that enjoyed by our fair Country-women, concerning which they hear me talk with wonder and incredulity. On one occasion a young lady observed to me that if the intercourse between the two sexes in my country was as unreserved as I represented it to be, the state of public morals must be very fine there. Could the most laboured detail give a better idea of the state of public morals here than such an observation from such a source? It is a thing almost unheard of in this Country for a young lady to go into any society unaccompanied by her Mamma, or some stiff and buckram-faced old aunt, and as to taking a walk with a Gentleman alone, Miss would think it a crime of such magnitude as to shrink at the bare idea. Ideas still *barer* do not however at all alarm her. Such is the force of education and habit, for waltzing is here looked upon as one of the most innocent amusements in the world, and a young lady who cannot brook being seen with a Gentleman on the public walk, thinks it as indifferent a thing as possible to clasp her hand on his shoulder, or perhaps one on each, and allow him to grasp her around the waist, and hold on pretty tightly too, and then dance round & round the room with him in this posture, intermingling knees between. Can anything be imagined more ridiculous and inconsistent? Yet the delicate minded old ladies look on without the least uneasiness, tho' they see their Daughters sometimes almost mooning in their partners' arms! The Europeans may flout as they will at the fastidiousness of the unpolished inhabitants of the other side of the Atlantic, but I hope and trust that region may remain long uncorrupted by such pernicious refinement, which cannot but have its effects in debasing the finest feeling of the soul.

The Russian nobility have adopted the foreign costume, but the other classes still adhere to their own. The national dress of women is, when they can afford it, very rich but at all events showy, & the Mosco costume beautiful. I have been at Balls where all have been apparelled in it, which happens but rarely, for the classes that adhere to them at the present day are not in the habit of frequenting balls. I am at a loss how to describe this Dress; it is kind of a Robe which buttons before all the way down to the ancles [sic] & is profusely embroidered, and bound with a broad ribbon or lace, it is mostly of some bright color, when not much bespangled, red I think the most becoming. Some of the young women wear Corsets but they do not brace them so tight as to punish or deform themselves as many of our ladies do. With this Dress they wear a kind of inverted crescent on their head, richly embroidered, and gradually tapering off toward the hidden part of the neck where it is tied with ribbon. Their Hair I must say is generally beautiful, and adorns them much, being for the most part a bright flax in color and worn hanging down their backs lower than their waists, neatly platted [sic] and tied with a ribbon near the end. In the winter they wear over their usual dress a kind of *long* short-Gown which covers their hips and is lined with fur, this too is rich if the owner can afford it, indeed the excessive diverseness of furs in this Country gives them an opportunity of displaying that extravagance which is said to be so natural to women, more in this garment than in any other, so that the part of their apparel which is only intended to protect them from the cold when in open air, is often worth thousands of Rubles.

I regret to say that nearly all the ladies here paint, and that very badly too, just as if you were to take some rouge on the end of your finger and rub a round spot on each cheek without caring at all for its being known. The Dress of the female Peasants is similar in shape to the one I have attempted to describe: and their gala suit very gay, so that it is no unpleasant thing to go through a large Russian village on a holiday and see them all clean, and in their best attire. These people however have a shocking disregard for the most beautiful part of the female form (which the mercantile class has not), so that in trying on their apron they tug their breasts down as low as they can which they confine under them in that disgusting position. The Consequence of this is, that in a short time they become much distended and softened, & upon the bosom of a young woman of twenty you see a pair of breasts which you would take to be the property of a Matron of sixty at least. It is in vain that I have endeavored to convince some of them of the folly of so revolting a fashion; they have always listened to me with great good nature but when I have ended my harangue, shaken their heads and said "*Niette batooshka lootchee tack.*"—No father, it is better thus.

The Russians though dirty in appearance, which arises chiefly from their seldom changing their clothes, are very fond of bathing and bathe often in all seasons: this is the case with both sexes and they seem upon pretty good terms with each other, for it isn't an uncommon thing to see men and women together in a River, or Bathouse. You will, of course, understand the lower classes. Such a sight however is far from recalling to mind those days of primitive simplicity when our ancestors are said to have partaken of this pleasure alike indiscriminately, on the contrary, it presents such a scene of barbarous degradation as cannot fail to inspire us with a very indifferent opinion of our species, it is an evidence of a nearer approach to the brute creation than we are willing to allow. What indeed can be imagined more brutal than the idea of seeing hundreds, you may say, of human beings of both sexes bathing together, and looking upon each other with the same indifference as a drove of cattle? We are but a sorry set of immortals at best I fear!

The national Baths are very singular things and struck me at first as being very ridiculous and indelicate, but habit reconciles us to everything, and when I lived in the Interior where I had one of them at my own lodgings (which is customary in the country in small towns) I became very fond of this mode of bathing & indulged in it often. The Russian bath has a large stove or *peech* in it, the room being very close, this peech is lit (as the term is) and serves at the same time to heat the apartment, and boil the water. The Process of bathing is as follows: the Person about to bathe, being stripped, lies down on a wide bench, which extends along each side of the room, and a man having put a stick of wood under his head proceeds to wash him. He takes a bucket of warm water into which he dips a piece [of] Mat, having first torn it to pieces, and filling the Mat well with soap, begins to rub and scrub his subject in the most unmerciful manner, turning him about from side to side just as if he were dead: in fact he goes through the whole operation with precisely the same degree of indifference that I have seen exhibited in washing cold and inanimate bodies. The lower classes of people, instead of pieces of Mat, use small branches of birch dried with the leaves on for this purpose, with which they beat one another til they become clean. This done the person must get up, and has water, first very warm, then tepid, then a little cooler, and finally as cold as he can bear it, poured upon his head, which running down his sides produces one of the most delightful and exquisite sensations I have experienced. In one corner of the room there is a higher bench erected where (the room being full of steam) it is naturally much warmer than below. On this bench or platform the Person lies after having been well washed and rinced [*sic*] and there enjoys in its highest perfection all the delicacy of the vapor Bath. The platform is so hot that the boards must be wetted with cold water before it is possible to support the situation. The Steam is produced by throwing water into a recess of the *peech*, upon an iron plate from whence it rushes in such a volume as for the moment almost to suffocate. There is certainly something very disagreeable and revolting in the idea of being rolled about and washed in the way I have described, by a great bearded fellow, and I insisted, the first time I went to one of these baths, on being shown into a Room where I might be quite alone; this shyness however soon wore off, and although I still take a private bath, I now never think of going into it unaccompanied. The Ladies are of course washed by women, and if a Gentleman be of such delicate nerves as to dislike being washed by a man, he has never any difficulty in procuring one of the "softer sex" willing to undertake that office, the honor and profit of this procuration devolve upon the *Banshtseek*, or attendant at the Baths. A Sopha or Mattress is always in an adjoining room.

In the Cities there are public baths of the Kind I have been describing where forty or fifty may bathe at a time, and as the Russians are not very fastidious in these matters they *do* bathe together to that number. There are usually two large apartments in them, one of which is properly speaking intended for the women, and one for the men, in case however of the former being visited by the latter, they do not appear in the least abashed nor discomfited. Adjoining the Bath House, there is generally a floored yard divided into two parts, one for each sex, where the very poorest people wash themselves in the open air during the summer season, branches being placed in it for their accomodation. No sight can be imagined more disgusting than the objects which are seen on going into the side devoted to females, as very old women repair thither in great numbers, who lank, haggard, and shrivelled up, offer a strange contrast to the immense masses of fat which are observed in women along side of them of a more moderate age. A young girl of a tolerably decent form serves sometimes to relieve the unseemly picture, but even among hundreds of *them* scarcely any are found worthy of notice, and none *on* whom the eye can dwell with pleasure. Had Thomson lived here the world would never have heard of Musidora. To wash one's self in the Department of the Bath last named costs 9^{co}, [kopecks] rather less than two cents our money, in the inner public apartments 50^{co}—the price of a bath in one of the private rooms is Rs [Rubles] 2.00 (& a few copecks to the *Banshtsheek.*), for this however, as many may bathe in it at a time as wish, say two, three or four. The Degree of heat common in one of these baths is said to be 40° of Reaumur, 120° Fahrenheit and the cold in the open air into which the Russians go without the least hesitation immediately after quitting the bath, is sometimes 30° of Reaumur, or 36° of Fahrenheit below zero. That so sudden a transition from one extreme to the other should not in many cases be attended with evil consequences it is difficult to believe: the fact admitted, it must serve as one of the strongest adducible instances of the force of habit; for the Russians are accustomed to this from their earliest childhood.

The Men in the Country may, many of them, be termed very fine looking men, but the passion for war being universal here you usually see them in a military coat (I speak of the High class) and as it is the fashion of the Russian officers to wear Corsets, they are mostly screwed up and distorted in the most ridiculous manner, so that it is no uncommon thing to see a young Man of 24 or 25 years of age, with a waist as thin as that of a Philadelphia lady, walking along half double, it being utterly impossible for him to hold himself strait. Some of course carry it to a greater excess than others. This contemptible and most vile and effeminate fashion extends even to the common soldiers who are all tortured in the same manner; with him however it does not probably proceed from choice.

Vanity is an inherent quality of the Russians, or rather an inherent failing; a failing which renders most nations contemptible in the eyes of their neighbours—among the Russians it is not confined to any rank nor degree, it is alike implanted in the breasts of the Peasant and the Prince, insomuch that although it must be acknowledged that this nation is far behind all others in Europe, or those sprung from European origin, yet the high opinion it entertains of itself gives it in its own conceit the most exalted station among them. The Poet expressed his pride in the glory and fine qualifications of his countrymen in the most unlimited and enthusiastic panegyric, whilst the vassal, abject as all vassals must be, thinks the guarantee of his honor quite sufficient in saying "Yah Roossky!" *I am a Russian,* and this too at the very moment he means to deceive you.

The following lines of one of their most celebrated Poets may serve as an illustration of the above Remark. The Translation is literal.

> O! Russian, O! mortal of magnanimous race,
> O! breast of stone,
> O! giant submissive to the Tsars,
> When and where couldst thou not attain
> Whatever glory was worthy of thee?
> Thy labours are to thee amusements;
> Thy crowns shine among the thunder clouds,
> Is the battle in the field? Thy brilliance
> obscures the starry vault,
> Is the war upon the waters? The abyss
> foams beneath thee,
> Thou art everywhere the terror of thy foes.
>
> Derjavin.

The Russian Merchants live very badly, indeed they do not know how to live well, though the rich ones have generally a large house, a fine horse, and, in Mosco, not infrequently a handsome wife. These things constituting what they consider luxury, neither is the idea at all amiss "in the abstract," but then they usually occupy some obscure & confined part of their house, and live upon coarse and common food. The Russian Merchant however gives a magnificent feast (if he can afford it) once or twice a year on his own & his wife's names' days in the observance of which they are very particular. If he be a man of sufficient importance to presume to do so, he invites to his entertainment some members of the nobility with whom

he may chance to be acquainted, and in case he should be honored by
their acceptance of his invitation, particularly if they be men of
importance, nothing can exceed the host's pride and gratitude. On
these occasions all the finest apartments, which in some houses are
very splendid, are thrown open, and every thing, however expensive,
is lavished upon his guests in the most extravagant and even ludicrous profusion. Champaign, Coffee, Chocolate, Tea, Malaga,
Burgundy, Sweetmeats of every species and preserved in the most
exquisite manner, Punches, Fruits of all kinds in the very dead of
Winter, of which a single dish sometimes costs thousands of Rubles;
in fact every thing is there that Luxury or extravagance can desire,
and handed about pretty much in the order I have mentioned; and
stuff yourself you must, above all if you should unfortunately happen
to be a stranger. Nothing can be imagined more dull and uninter-
esting, "weary, stale, flat, & unprofitable," than one of these Evening
societies in a Merchant's house, although they only assemble as I
have already observed once or twice a year, and might therefore be
reasonably supposed to be overburdened with a store of scandal and
anecdote. The men lounge about and play cards, and the women sit
in a room by themselves, stuck up for all the world like painted dolls,
devoid of all spirit and animation. This lasts to perhaps one or two
o'clock in the Morning, when not withstanding all the foregoing
stuffing, a prodigious supper is served up, two or three hours long,
at which they sit and cram themselves again till they are ready to
burst. The Champaign, in which the health of the master & the
mistress of house is drunk, is handed around by a servant, and all
the guests must drink out of the same glass; this is what they call
living together, *droojestvo*, or in a friendly way. The sweetmeats are,
in like manner, set out on a side table, with but one spoon in each
saucer, at which whoever feels inclined takes a lick, and puts it
back again for the accomodation of his successor. These things, by
the bye, are practised in the houses of the first nobility, and
universally practised too. I have never seen the sweetmeat part of
the Concern managed differently. I have counted at one of the
suppers above described twenty three various dishes handed around
one after another. Some people say they have seen fifty on similar
occasions—I can not vouch for a greater number than twenty three.

Some, instead of Evening Parties and Suppers, give Dinners equally splendid and profuse, they not failing in either case, to display enormous and masif services of plate, which they are in the habit of borrowing from their friends, in order to give their entertainments a greater degree of *eclat*.

The nobility on the other hand live well at all times, and their politeness and hospitality exceed all bounds; on entering their houses the manner in which every thing is offered gives the fullest assurance that you are a welcome visitor, and in the interior of the country where they are little tainted by foreign manners, they are in fact the most excellent and unsophisticated people. I lived for some time on the estate of one of them, between 5 & 600 versts from this place, and never once abroad have I been treated with so much attention and kindness. I had, during my residence in the neighbourhood, many invitations from people of great rank to spend the whole Summer with them, but could not avail myself of their offers, my object not being exactly pleasure.

The Religion of the Russians is that of the Greek Church; there are however several sects who differ from each other in some of their tenets; the service is performed among them all in the Sclavonian language, and their mode of worship abounds in forms and ceremonies. Their churches are adorned with rich altars, and many images of the saints, the holy Virgin, and Christ, some of which are very valuable in consequence of the diamonds and precious stones by which they are surrounded. (There is one of the holy Virgin in the great Cathedral in Mosco, said to be painted by St. Luke, estimated at several millions of Rubles.) There are no seats in their churches the want of which is but little felt, in as much as there is very seldom any preaching. The Priests are remarkable for their fine hair, which they wear hanging loosely down their backs to a considerable length, combed and curled in the nicest manner. They are mostly poor, and men without influence except in the affairs of the Church—their moral character is not understood to be irreproachable, they cannot however be charged with indulging immoderately in what we consider the good things of this work.

I must now, Sir, beg leave to conclude, which is a privilege you will no doubt allow me with little reluctance. My Remarks have been spun out, in copying, to a much greater length than I first intended: if they should afford you any gratification in their perusal, I shall be highly flattered; if on the contrary they should only serve to weary your patience, I must beg a thousand pardons for having put your good nature to so severe and tedious a trial.

Believe me to be very respectfully and sincerely

your friend.
Wm. D. Lewis

A COUNTRY SALOON

MAN OF THE "BLACK PEOPLE"—
THE LOWER CLASSES

TEA-SELLERS IN THE STREETS

DROSKY DRIVERS

10 ASIATIC MAGNIFICENCE AND EUROPEAN CIVILIZATION

Alexander Hill Everett (1790–1847)

Alexander Hill Everett, who had worked in the law office of John Quincy Adams, accompanied him as private secretary when Adams was appointed the first American minister to the czarist government. His two years as an attaché of the legation of St. Petersburg (1809–1810) were for Everett the start of a diplomatic career in Europe. Based on this experience he published several books on European affairs. For some years he also edited the *North American Review* in his native Boston.

His post in St. Petersburg provided Everett entry into the circles of the Russian aristocracy. He was highly impressed by their gracious social life, and, therefore, he did not fear that Russia's military and political influence in Europe would threaten the survival of Western culture. To the contrary, he was not adverse to Russian predominance in Western Europe. As he pointed out in 1822 in a book on the political situation in Europe, from which the following pages have been excerpted,[83] Russian rule in Western Europe would only represent a change of power from one cultured upper class to another. It would not signify, as others feared, the subjection of European civilization to the rule of a semibarbarian people from the east.

———————————

THE PROMINENT FEATURE in the immediate future prospects of Europe . . . is the probable prevalence of the influence and arms of

Russia on the western nations. It remains, therefore, to inquire what will be the effect of this event, should it happen, upon the state of civilization and the establishment of a general government.

If the Russian influence in the west of Europe were decidedly unfavorable to the progress of civilization, it would check in the same degree the tendency towards political union resulting from this progress. And as the mass of the Russian people is now in a very uncivilized state, it may appear, at first view, as if this would in fact be the consequence. But farther reflection may perhaps lead to a different opinion. The prevalence of Russian power is not the prevalence of rude barbarians, that constitute the bulk of the nation, but of the dominant class of proprietors, which is equally civilized with the same class in any other part of Europe. Their political influence, as far as it affects the body of society, would be exerted in the same direction, and produce the same consequences, as that of the authorities now existing. It will doubtless be, for a considerable period of time to come, the immediate interest of this class in Russia, to check the development of civilization, in one of its particular forms, viz. that of liberal political institutions. Their whole exertions are now employed for this purpose; and it is under this pretext, as I have observed, that they will gradually extend their political and military power on other countries. But this effort, in reality, counteracts itself; and the persecution of liberal ideas only increases the ardor, with which they are embraced and propagated. This temporary pressure will therefore serve to prepare the way, at some future period, for violent explosions in favour of liberty. Meanwhile, the Russian influence counteracts, in another way, its own efforts in favour of arbitrary principles, by the strong encouragement which is given to the development of civilization, in every other branch, except the modification of political forms. The Russian nobles, who are doubtless the wealthiest proprietors in Europe, are also among the most active and munificent patrons of industry. In their private and social habits, as individuals, they unite the gorgeous magnificence of Asia with the fine taste of the western world, and encourage, by consumption of their products, the luxurious and elegant arts, more than perhaps any other class of persons whatever.

There is something like enchantment in the height of perfection, to which this new nation has carried, as it were in a moment, all the graces and accomplishments of social life; and the aristocracy of Europe no where exhibits itself under so favourable a point of view, as in Russia, because it there adds to the refinement, which distinguishes the same class in other countries, a lofty magnanimity of character resulting from the secure possession of unbounded wealth and unlimited power; advantages which the aristocracy elsewhere have either wholly lost, or live in the daily expectation of losing. The Russian nobles speak with the finished elegance the most cultivated tongues of the west of Europe, and are familiar with the polite literature of France, Italy and Germany. The splendours of their princely palaces, surrounded with parks and lawns, in the finest state of gardening, and furnished with the costliest products of the taste and skill of the west of Europe, their collections of pictures and statuary from the workshops of the most celebrated masters, their large and valuable repositories of books and manuscripts in all the languages of the world, their stores of wealth in the various departments of natural science, their astonishing exhibition of civilization springing up in the full luxuriant bloom of its highest perfection from a soil still completely barbarous, their union of fine taste and various accomplishments with the adventitious lustre of social distinctions and boundless fortune; all this strikes very powerfully upon the imagination and rather seems to realize the brilliant fables of eastern romance, than to resemble the actual condition of any other society that ever existed. The scientific taste of these great proprietors is far from being a matter of parade and charlantry. The botanical garden of prince Razumofsky, near Moscow, is probably superior to any other private collection in the world; and we have seen the illustrous chancellor, count Romanzoff, fitting out at his own expense a voyage of discovery round the globe; and giving at the same time a singular proof of toleration, by erecting upon one of his principal estates three churches on the same square, appropriated respectively to the Greek, Catholic and Jewish communions, for the use of his tenants and subjects. The attention of these nobles, as a body politic, or, in other words, that of the government, has also been steadily directed towards the promotion of literature and science; and with the magnanimity naturally resulting from their social position, they exhibited a singular liberality in their political ideas, until occurrences abroad had shown, that this system was too contrary to their immediate interest.

The influence of such a society over the west of Europe is not, therefore, the inroad of a horde of barbarians under an Attila or an Omar, which sweeps away in its progress every trace of improvement. It is merely a change of power from the hands of one cultivated and civilized government to those of another, and will produce no unfavourable effect on the state of society. On the contrary, as its immediate operation would be to increase the intercourse between the other parts of Europe and Russia, it would at once accelerate the progress of improvement in this vast region, and, by so doing, give an additional stimulus from abroad to the same principle in the west.

A RUSSIAN TROIKA

CLERGY OF THE RUSSIAN CHURCH

11 LA BÊTE À FACE HUMAINE

Henry Middleton (1770–1846)

Henry Middleton served as the American minister to Russia during a period both interesting and critical from the point of view of internal Russian developments and that of American-Russian relations. Appointed by President Monroe in 1820, he held that office at the time of the declaration of the Monroe Doctrine in 1823 and during the Decembrist Conspiracy of 1825. Prior to his appointment he had been active in South Carolina politics and had served as governor of the state and also as a member of the United States Congress.

As a young man Middleton had witnessed the convulsions of the French Revolution. This may have awakened in him a distrust of revolutionary upheavals and influenced his view of the Decembrists' attempt at a change in Russia, as reflected in his dispatch of January 30, 1826, which follows.[84] While acknowledging the need for reforms, Middleton lacked confidence in the ability of the masses to participate in government. Thus he held that absolutism was the only viable form of rule in Russia.

•━━━━━━━━━━━━━━━━━━━━━━━━━━━•

IT WILL NOT be denied that a reform is become generally necessary throughout the state, not only on account of the intolerable abuses which exist, but the doctrines preached up in the West have given an impulse even in Russia towards a better order of things. Yet such is the besotted ignorance prevailing throughout the great mass to whom the physical force belongs, and so glimmering is the intelligence possessed by those who domineer over it, that a struggle between these classes would be truly disastrous in its consequences, and such

87

a catastrophe should therefore be avoided with the greatest caution, and no measure capable of provoking it be adopted.

The Corps of Noblesse (including the military) is the only portion of the population which may be deemed civilized; and of course alone can be considered as an element entering into any political or moral calculation. The rest of the mass, or 19/20 of the whole, is really little more than what it has been harshly denominated, "La Bête à face humaine." Indeed it enjoys no other but a physical existence and cannot therefore be ripe for the apportion or maintenance of its undoubted rights. . . .

However startling the assertion may appear at first, it can be shown from the history of this government, that the great *arcanum Imperii* —that which its statesmen have long considered and do still consider to be its *Palladium*—is the doctrine of *Absolutism*; and the opinion is perhaps not erroneous which holds this to be the only principle which can bind together so heterogeneous a mass as is aggregated under the sceptre of the Russian autocrat.

If it be true that Despotism can never long flourish except in a barbarous nation, it seems equally certain that no other form but the despotic can maintain itself in the same circumstances. Suffice it then to remark that *these*, as regards the great mass of the nation, are yet unchanged in Russia.

If any feasible means were discoverable whereby the benefits of civil liberty would be immediately secured to the population of Russia, the Emperor Alexander, who is known to have valued the absolute power he swayed only as the means of doing good, would assuredly have attempted it. But such is the force of circumstances and such the power of surrounding influences that he was seldom able to carry into effect any reform however inconsiderable in his hereditary dominions. All the persons who have profited, do profit or expect to profit by abuses (and a most numerous class they are) must be enemies of reform. All the superior classes of society too in this country, have confirmed habits of domination, as difficult to break, but not more so, than the correspondent habits of slavish obedience in the inferior. Whether or not it was from a just view and experience of the difficulties to be encountered in all the attempts at reform, the fact is certain, that the late Emperor's inclination towards liberalism had very much diminished of late years. His attempts too at giving a Constitution to Poland seem to have succeeded so little to his expectation, that there appeared latterly very little disposition in him to perfect his work by putting that Constitution into full execution. The last *additional act* (closing the doors of the legislative Chamber) looked very like a desire of undoing what had already been effected. Great allowances ought however to be made for the influence of the neighbouring Powers who all seem to have considered the institutions granted to this country as working injury.—

An inquiry of deep interest to foreign nations is what are the future prospects of Russia under the autocracy, and will she enjoy an existence sufficiently tranquil at home to permit her to exercise a commanding influence abroad? I incline rather to the opinion, that the habit of obedience is so firmly established, that but little management is required to keep all in the subjection which is become a kind of second nature. Add to this that it seems most natural that the present body of the Nobility should incline to bear with the autocracy placed above it, in order to enjoy the benefits of the *servage* beneath it. While on the other hand the Crown, however disposed, from many considerations both moral and political, to elevate the condition of the serf, will yet be careful not to do anything which shall tend to change the relations by means of which the autocracy is rendered so necessary in the state. To the second part of the inquiry it may be answered, that if Russia enjoys peace within her own dominions, the degree of influence she will exercise abroad must depend upon the will backed by the ability of those who shall be placed at the head of a nation possessing such vast resources.

After all however, it would bespeak an extreme rashness, to confide in any prognostic of tranquillity in a nation where under the reign of a prince like Alexander, various conspiracies were matured undiscovered, and *thirteen* different individuals (most of whom were officers) could be found to volunteer their services to accomplish his destruction.

12 RUSSIA'S FUTURE COURSE FAVORS THE BEST INTERESTS OF HUMANITY

George Bancroft (1800–1891)

George Bancroft, prominent in politics and diplomacy, is best remembered as a great American historian. A sober, serious New England youth, he studied in Europe from 1818 to 1823 with many of the great minds of his age. When he returned to the United States, a man of the world who showed in speech and manner how much he had overcome the provincialism of his early years, his erstwhile mentor at Harvard, Elliot Norton, turned away from him in disgust and refused to speak with him for years.

As a historian Bancroft neglected the social and economic factors in favor of a broad philosophical view, one that he may have acquired from his German teachers. He saw history in terms of progress and liberation of the masses. This historical perspective is evident in his essay on Russia written in 1829, from which the following pages have been excerpted.[85] Bancroft—who, incidentally, had never been to Russia—was not concerned, as he said, with the "barbarous details" of early Russian history, the superstition of the masses and the excesses of the nobles, because "the history of the future cannot be read in the experience of the past." Instead he addressed himself to what he saw as the incipient manifestations of a great Russian national development.

●————————————————————————————●

RUSSIA FORMS a connecting link between ancient and modern history. France, Spain, and England, were all conquered, and adopted the manners, the dialect, and the learning of their conquerors. In the heart of Germany, the Teutonic race preserved itself free from the loss of its language and its nationality. Have not the nations of Teutonic descent proved, by the results of their influence on human events and intelligence, that, as a mercy and a benefit to the world, their name and nation were preserved unsubdued and unmixed? Have not some of the most valuable principles in learning, in philosophy, in religion, and, we may add, in the imaginative arts, been the results of their independence? Though it was long before they learned to unite the elegances of other times with native dignity and the acquisitions of knowledge, yet have they not at last shown themselves strong in the depth of sentiment, in earnest truth, and moral sublimity? And is it going too far to hope, that one branch of the great Sclavonic family is yet to develop an independent character; that a nation, which has its unity and identity confirmed and endeared by a community of language, of religious faith, and of historical recollections,—a nation placed on lands which join the Caspian and White Sea, the Baltic, and the most important basin of the Mediterranean,—a nation occupying a soil intersected by the largest rivers of Europe, and offering great and increasing facilities of navigation by canals,—a nation which reaches from the country of the vine and olive, to the latitudes of perpetual frost, and thus unites within itself all the conditions of national strength, commercial independence, and intellectual energy,—is it unreasonable to trust that the future course of such a nation is to be marked by results favorable to the best interests of humanity? That its copious and harmonious language is to become the voice of the muses, and the instrument of science? That culture is to find a way into its healthful and fertile valleys, and that religion and civil liberty are eventually to win new trophies in these immense regions of ancient darkness? The Russian empire, like the United States, if comparatively weak for purposes of foreign aggression, is invincible within itself. Its soil is capable of sustaining, without supposing an uncommon degree of culture, a population of a hundred and fifty millions; the most vigorous government may find enough to do in controlling the members of this vast body politic; the most ambitious can have within its limits the means of gratifying an unwearied activity. It already covers a vaster extent of territory than any which the annals of the world commemorate, except it be the transitory dominion of the Zingis. When every motive of philanthropy, and of the true passion for glory, impels to the diffusion of sciences, the full display of the great and good qualities which exist in the ancient race that has held the north from immemorial ages, it seems not an unreasonable expectation, that the voice of humanity and justice will be heard. It may be within the purposes of a controlling Providence, that the agency of the Russian empire shall spread respect for Christianity through the hearts of idolatrous nations. Its emissaries have already reared the temples of a purer religion among the Tartar states of Siberia, and planted the cross on the mountains of Kamchatka. The traveller, as he wanders towards the pole, in latitudes where corn is ripened in a day (day that stretches over weeks), hears the sounds, and sees the character of a Christian worship; and monasteries are established even in the remote isles of the White Sea; the shores of the Caspian have ceased to acknowledge a Mohametan master, and the ancient fable of the prisoner of Mount Caucasus, the purest and most sublime invention of ancient mythology, has been but the faint shadowing forth of more glorious truths, which are making themselves felt and acknowledged in the very heart of the mysterious land of classic superstition.

But if, on the contrary, the form of autocracy should prove incompatible with the diffusion of knowledge, and if Russia should fail to attain to a government insuring the free development of national energy and the strict accountability of public servants, there may ensure a new migration of nations and a subversion of ancient order, like the terrible devastations of the great destroyer of the middle ages. What force could the western nations oppose to the gradual advancement of Russian supremacy? The capital of Poland is nearly the centre of Europe, and it is in the hands of the Russians; Austria has possessions which are said to sigh for the yoke of the Sclavonic masters, rather than yield allegience to the house of Hapsburg; Russia holds the ports through which provinces of the mighty state have their intercourse with the sea; and probably the prosperity of both parts would be promoted by a union of the seaports and the interior under a stronger government. The Wallachians, the

Moldavians, are of the same religious faith. It is not many years since Europe shrieked at the aggressions of Poland; yet now a large part of the old Polish provinces rejoice in being re-united to their ancient brethren; the heart of the kingdom, the grand duchy of Warsaw, has not for centuries enjoyed such tranquillity, such security, or such general prosperity, as at present; the Polish provinces of Prussia lament their separation from their fellow-citizens of the old republic. Where, then, is the barrier against Russia on her frontiers? On the north, she extends to the poles, and the conquest of Finland has made her inaccessible from the Scandinavian peninsula; on the east, her limit is the Pacific, unless, indeed, we take into account her possessions in North America. On the south, she is herself most formidable to every one of her neighbors. Caucasian countries and the keys of Persia are already hers; no vessels sail on the Caspian but by her permission; she holds more than half of the Black Sea; the Turkish power may yet shine forth in temporary lustre before it expires; but religion and national enthusiasm and personal bravery, cannot resist the influence of causes which are constantly operating, and always increasing in strength. Thus, Russia, inaccessible on the south, east, and north, stands in a menacing attitude towards the south-east and the west of Europe. Did not Peter the Great wish to become a state of the German empire? Has not a part of the Baltic coast belonging to Prussia been repeatedly grasped at? Did not the wise, the temperate, the forbearing Alexander, accept from his suffering and prostrate ally a portion of coveted territory in Galicia? Did he not, even after the peace of Tilsit, partake in the spoils of his unhappy associate in arms? The memory of these things has not perished; has justice entrenched herself in firmer sanctuaries? Has the consciousness of moral obligation so far gained force, that the appearance of a tyrant on a powerful throne would no longer perplex monarchs with a fear of change?

The statesman that believes in human virtue, may still seek for a guarantee of right in permanent interests, and in sufficient strength to repel unjust aggressions. It is painful to suppose that the balance of power in the north is so far destroyed, that the strongest hope of security lies in the wisdom of governments, the personal virtues of sovereigns, and the cordial union of the weaker nations.

But it is said that the Russian empire is a huge mass, which will of itself fall asunder. And why will it fall asunder? Is there not the tie of kindred in the great nucleus of the empire? Is not the whole well annealed and firmly joined? Is it not cut off and separated from the rest of Christendom by its peculiar church discipline? Is it not one and undivided by its descent? Is it not bound together by having the same military heroes, the same saints, the same recollections, civil and sacred? Next to France, it is of all the states of Europe the one which is safest against division. How much more secure in its unity is Russia than Austria, which yet is secure except from some general convulsion. Of the Poles, the Russians, the Hungarians, the Bohemians, the Germans, the Illyrians, and the Italians which by their motley union constitute the ill-assorted mosaic of the great central souvereignty, how many at present dislike the Austrian supremacy! Will Hungary submit to be a dependency of a country of far less natural resources? Will the beautiful and fertile Bohemia consent to the annihilation of its language, of its national laws and constitutions, its time-honored liberties? Will Russians prefer the sway of a foreign power to sharing the glory of their kindred? Will Poles desire to remain divided from Poles? Prussia labors under infinitely greater danger of dismemberment than Russia. The idea, that Russia of itself will break in pieces, is unfounded in the history or the character of the component parts of that empire.

But still it is so vast, so unwieldy!—And is it more easy to tear a member from the leviathan than a fly? Are the limbs of the beast less firmly knit, because they are huge and massive? It is a clear lesson of history that large states hold together, long after wisdom has departed from the councils of their governors. The Roman empire never fell till it was shaken from abroad. The Greek empire lasted a thousand years longer, and would, in all probability, have lasted to this day, had it not received an irresistible shock from a nation which as yet had no home. Now the danger which is said to hang over Russia is solely from within itself.

The history of the future cannot be read in the experience of the past. We may trust that the new relations, which are rising in the world, will yet lead to a balance of power, dependent on the moral force of intelligence. We can but hope that a bright and peaceful futurity awaits a government on which depends directly the happiness of sixty millions of men, a fifteenth part of the human race; a government which holds under its sway a large part of the habitable globe; a government whose soil is susceptible of infinite improvements, and whose population is but just beginning to bear some reasonable proportion to its natural abundance. The voice of Sclavonic poetry has already been heard, and the lessons of the Russian bards are full of the noblest truths. The Russian press is active. Works on domestic history are multiplying. The spirit of the nation is aroused by the recollections which go back for so many centuries. The pride of national feeling is deep and strong, and arts and letters are making their way into the heart of a country which from its earliest ages has possessed an aptitude for learning.

Nor should it be left out of view, that while the general administration is autocratic, the municipal regulations are free; that local customs, constitutions, and religious peculiarities are preserved; and that, while there is no legitimate guarantee of civil liberty, and no exact limit to check the infringement of the imperial authority on particular privileges, yet practically the local institutions are respected; and in an autocracy, of which the territory is immense, the hand of the sovereign is not felt in its rudeness except in his personal vicinity.

It is in a small kingdom that a tyrant is the most dreaded monster. In a large state the personal vices of the sovereign extend in their direct influence hardly beyond his immediate train.

They who limit their attention in Russian annals to anecdotes which illustrate the debauchery of the court, the ignorance of the nobles, or the superstitions of the vulgar, close their eyes on one of the greatest spectacles. The reception of the Russians into the pale of civilized Christendom forms an epoch in civilization, so wide are its influences, so powerful, grand, and beneficent the consequences to which it has led or may lead. How different would have been the future of the world if the Russian state with its present power had adopted the manners and the religion of the east? What safety would there now be to Christian Europe? What increased dangers would not hang over its liberties? He that can neglect such results in the delineation of strange and uncouth manners or in the scandalous chronicles of the licentiousness of an immoral court, gives up the contemplation of the great revolutions in national destinies, to the unworthy office of analyzing the vices of individual profligates. One of the noblest branches of knowledge, the history of nations, loses its dignity and value.

13 THE RUSSIANS ARE DISTINGUISHED FOR GENIUS, ENTERPRISE, AND COURAGE

United States Magazine and Democratic Review
Washington

John O'Sullivan, who first publicized the term of America's Manifest
Destiny, founded the *United States Magazine and Democratic Review*
in 1837. In November 1842 it was combined with Orestes A.
Brownson's *Boston Quarterly Review*. The journal, partisan to
Andrew Jackson and van Buren, took a middle-of-the-road stand on
slavery. Literary essays combined with excellent articles on political,
social, and economic questions made it an important journal.

In 1842, when a "Recent Visiter" [sic] published the following
"New Notes on Russia" in the magazine,[86] relations between Russia
and the United States were not affected by the existing Anglo-Russian
tensions that in the next decade would lead to the Crimean War.

•————————————————————————————•

IT IS ALMOST dangerous to say anything favorable of the Russians,
so universal is the opinion in Europe, and in America too, that they
are a nation of ignorant and savage barbarians, not susceptible to
civilization, and fit only for the brutal bondage in which we are told
they are still held. These impressions arise from travels written a
century ago, copied by succeeding travellers, even to the present
time; from the monthly fabrications of English and French journalists, who find it a profitable business to abuse Russia and the
Russians; and from hasty opinions formed by discontented travellers,
who fly, as fast as they can, through a country where they find few

97

good roads or public conveyances, soft beds, or comfortable inns. The American traveller, as he passes through their villages and towns, and sees the Russian peasants clothed in sheep-skins and sleeping in groups upon the pavements, is strongly reminded of the savages of our wilderness, and imagines them equally benighted. But those who will take the trouble to inform themselves will learn that the Russian Slavonians, though held in vassalage for centuries, are naturally distinguished for genius, enterprise, courage, devotion to their country, an unwavering fidelity to their vows, and a devout reverence for their church. There are innumerable instances of inventions and mechanical works of serfs who could neither read nor write. At the present time the instructed serfs are employed in every branch of trade and industry—in every art and science. This was in some measure the case even in the last century. We are told by the Count of Ségur, who was the Minister of France in the time of Catherine II, that on her return from her celebrated expedition to the Crimea, Count de Cheremetieff gave a splendid entertainment at his beautiful villa near Moscow, on which occasion there was an opera and ballet. He says that the architect who constructed the hall for the opera, the painter who ornamented it, the poet and the musicians, the authors of the opera, the performers in it and in the ballet, were all serfs of the Count de Cheremetieff. The peasants are also remarkable for their superstitious courage. On more occasions than one have the Russian troops been slaughtered by an overpowering force, refusing to obey the order to retreat, in consequence of some vow that they would not turn their backs upon the enemy. Their conduct in abandoning Moscow in 1812—following their priests with the sacred symbols of their religion, chanting hymns of lamentation, and invoking the aid of heaven,—as the scene is described by the French historian of that disastrous campaign—was characteristic of the self-sacrificing devotion of the Russians to their country. . . .

Most travellers take it for granted that all these peasants are not only in a state of deplorable ignorance but of abject slavery. This is not so. About one third, as is estimated, pay an annual hire to their masters or to the crown, and are employed as merchants, tradesmen, mechanics, architects, nay, in every branch of industry, art and science; some of them are wealthy, and some distinguished for their skill and talents. Such is the condition of this portion of the serfs. It is supposed that about another third are on the crown lands. These pay an annual quit-rent to the crown, and enjoy the produce of their own labor. They are virtually mere tenants of the crown, and are in as good a condition as any peasantry in Europe. The remaining third are on the lands of the nobility. Even these would be quite as well off as most of the peasantry in neighboring nations, if the laws for their protection were executed. According to these they cannot be sold without the land; their punishment is regulated; they are required to labor only three days for their master and three for themselves, on land which the master must set apart for their use. But these laws are evaded or violated; and, on badly managed estates particularly, the condition of the serf is wretched indeed. It may well be imagined what must be the condition of this portion of the peasantry of Russia in times of famine, when a single proprietor, perhaps without any property but his lands and serfs, and without credit, is called upon suddenly to supply food for the ten, twenty, thirty, forty, nay up to 150,000.

WORKMEN OF NOVGOROD—GLAZIER, PAINTER, AND CARPENTERS

MERCHANTS' SLEIGHS COMING FROM THE IRBÍT FAIR

MERCHANT AND FAMILY—FISH PEDDLER

14 TWO GREAT NATIONS, GUARANTORS OF WORLD PEACE

Charles Stewart Todd (1791–1871)

Charles Stewart Todd was appointed minister to Russia by President Tyler and served from 1841 to 1845, a period without major problems between the two countries. Born in Kentucky, the son of a jurist who later became an associate justice at the Supreme Court, he followed in his father's footsteps, practicing law in Lexington. During the war of 1812 he served on the staff of General William H. Harrison and rose to the rank of colonel. He entered politics, and in later life he devoted himself to business.

Todd's remarks on Russia, which follow, were made in a speech given in 1846.[87] They are optimistic about the relationship between Russia and the United States, two powers "destined to be the best neighbors, because they are so far off."

THE FIRST IMPRESSION that strikes the traveller, on entering St. Petersburg, is directed to the deep, clear river, noble quarries of granite with iron railings, splendid streets, magnificent palaces, and the hundred churches with lofty spires and guilded domes; and he then turns with astonishment from these monuments of civilization, to look at the people who have reared them—serfs, with their long beards, clad in sheep-skin coats with the wool inside. The resources of Russia are of vast extent; independently of the productions of her soil and of her workshops, &c., she has great mineral wealth; gold, platina, copper, and iron abound in greater quantities than in any other portion of Europe, if not of the globe; though no mines of coal are to be found. The consumption of this article, at St. Petersburg, is supplied as ballast in the ships, and is as cheap as at New Castle. In her geographical position so compact; in her military capacities, in her warlike character, and her vast energies, concentrated by the genius of one mind, Russia may be regarded as the first Northern power in Europe, if not the equal of any on the Continent. Like our own beloved land, she is the child of the eighteenth century. In the last hundred years she has advanced as rapidly as her neighbors in all that constitutes the strength of a State, if we except the results which flow only from the diffusion of intelligence among the masses. Like our own country, she is formidable in her offensive, as well as defensive attitude: she by her isolated position and gigantic army; we by our extended coast and efficient marine. Under a proper system of culture, she, like the United States, possesses ample means for feeding her own people, and of contributing to the wants of other nations,—in all substantial respects, the two powers are the most independent on the globe. They have no conflicting points of contact; they are destined to be the best neighbors, because they are so far off. The power of steam is working wonders in both; railroads will give them permanent tranquillity, for in the concentrated means of war are found the surest guarantees of peace. The capacity which their internal facilities afford for precipitating a large military force from the interior to the frontier will preserve both from invasion, while, in Russia, the vast railroad contemplated by the Emperor, for uniting the Baltic with the Black Sea and the Caspian, will give him the power to invade the contiguous nations at the same time his standing army, permitted from this power of sudden concentration to be reduced in numbers and expenses, is engaged in preserving the public peace at home. With this interesting nation we have always maintained a friendly intercourse. It is a sublime spectacle, worthy the contemplation of other powers, to see two great nations, the most extensive in territory and resources, in the Old and in the New World, always living in peace. As to them, the Temple of Janus has been always shut; may it never be opened! And may I not renew to you an expression of the sentiment in which, with the independence and courtesy of a Kentuckian, I indulged in my last interview with the Emperor, that the day might soon arrive when the power of the United States and Russia, by sea and by land, should be such as to command all nations of the earth to be at peace.

15 POLITICS IS A VERY COOL AND CALM BUSINESS

New York Herald

During political and military crises in mid-nineteenth-century Europe, such as the revolutions of 1848–1849 and the Crimean War of 1853–1856, American opinion wavered between condemnation and approval of Russian policies. Generally, Americans stood on the side of European liberalism against reactionary Russian despotism and Russia's suppression of national movements allied with the liberal forces. Public sentiment shifted to the support of Russia, however, when there was a danger that the Western powers, England and France, might gain the upper hand to an extent that could enable them to eliminate Russian influence in European affairs. Americans seemed to prefer a European balance of power with neither Russia nor the allied powers having undisputed hegemony. A victorious Russia, having crushed the liberal forces in Europe and dominating the Eastern Hemisphere from the Atlantic to the Pacific, could represent a serious threat to the United States. But so could a victory of England and France, since both countries maintained bases and interests in the Western Hemisphere.

The frequent shifts and contradictions following from these considerations found eloquent expressions in the editorial pages of the *New York Herald*, a paper that, it has been said, "cared little for principle and was apt to change its opinions frequently to meet the shifts in popular thinking. . . . The *Herald* had . . . few fixed ideas. There was perhaps only one idea which it invariably supported—that of American imperialism. It was chauvinistic and imperialistic always."[88] At the time, moreover, it was the American newspaper with the largest and best staff of foreign correspondents. It was also the most articulate on matters of European and world affairs.

To justify its position of the moment, the *Herald* often used arguments of an ideological or religious nature. But it did not always try to conceal the factor that determined its vacillating attitude—the potential or actual threat to American interests. These interests extended both to Europe and the Far East. They were not bound up with the one or the other of the contending European powers. In April of 1849 the *Herald* favored Christian Russia against Mohammedan Turkey, disregarding a possible Russian threat to the liberal forces in Europe, which were under great pressure by the European monarchies. In that same month, however, the Hungarians rebelled against Austria and were crushed by that monarchy with Russia's support. The Hungarian cause was very popular in the United States, which is reflected in the *Herald*'s hostile stance against Russia in the editorial of June 8, 1849. In 1852, the *Herald* predicted that sometime in the future Russia and the United States would enter into a direct conflict and that a decisive battle would be fought in the Far East, not in Europe.

When the Crimean War broke out in 1853, however, editorial opinion supported Russia against the Western powers, shifting once again at the conclusion of that war in 1856. Accepting Russia's defeat, the *Herald* now looked toward a *modus vivendi* with England and France. While their threat to American hegemony in the Western Hemisphere was real enough, the war had shown the limits of their military strength, too, especially when operating at a large distance from the home bases. "Cool" and "calm" were the words with which the *Herald* ended its reports on this episode.

SUPPOSE RUSSIA SHOULD subjugate Turkey in Europe, and passing over into Asia, prosecute her conquests, would the result be disastrous to civilization and humanity? Would the subjection of the ancient abodes of learning and civilization in the East, to this great Northern power, be so frightful a calamity? We do not believe that it would be a calamity. On the contrary, we are inclined to think that, in this onward movement of Russia, which must, to all appearance now, sooner or later, end in the conquest of the Ottoman empire, may be discerned the tokens of the speedy extinction of that system of idolatry, superstition, and semi-barbarism which has clouded the destinies of Asia for a long period. The barbarous fanaticism of the Turks can be exterminated only by a war of semi-religious conquest. Just by such a rude discipline as that of the Russian sword, can such a system of inhumanity, barbarism, and false religion, as that of the Turkish empire, be exterminated, and the elements of civilization and the Christian faith be introduced in its stead. . . . The crescent will give way to the Cross. Mohametan mosques will become Christian sanctuaries.—The imposture of the Prophet will be succeeded by the true faith, and the way opened up for the ultimate subjection of the whole region over which the ancient eastern Roman empire extended, to the sway of Christian civilization.

There is much grandeur in the prospect which this view of the Russian policy unveils. With whatever alarm, then, the course of Russia may strike the supporters of other European dynasties, we can see no reason why the subjugation of Turkey to that power should be regarded as calamitous to the interests of liberty and civilization. It would be at once an imposing and gratifying spectacle to behold the ancient abodes of learning and refinement in the East —from which we derived the first elements of our system of civilization—re-conquered from the blaspheming Turk, and freed from the corrupting and debasing influences of Mohametanism. As for the dangers which may threaten popular liberty from the vast accession to the power of the Russian empire, which these Eastern conquests would produce, we do not fear them. As in Rome it was esteemed the mark of a good citizen never to despair of the republic, so, in this latter day of more perfect light and liberty, we shall not fear for the permanent stability of those great principles of civil and religious liberty before whose conquering progress the despotisms of ages are crumbling away, while kings and princes, a bye-word and a mockery, are calling on the mountains and the rocks to cover them. This grand movement of Russia towards the East, is but one step towards the emancipation of that region of the globe from the worst species of thraldom. [April 21, 1849]

In this mighty drama, with France at the head of the liberal cause, and Russia leading the despots, what position will be taken by the liberal and enlightened governments of England and the United States. . . . Ought not the foreign policy of the American government . . . to be such as to give all the weight of its influence, advice and activity in favor of France, in the approaching struggle with Russia? . . .

Suppose France should succumb in the approaching struggle— suppose Russia, with her armies joined with the armies of Austria and Prussia, after having crushed Hungary, after having put down all the little States of Germany, after having buried the liberties of Italy beneath the bodies of millions of the brave, butchered, hung, drawn and quartered, shot down, hung up like dogs, for daring to think of liberty—suppose, after all this, the great Russian confederacy of monarchs should succeed finally in putting down republicanism in France—then, when all Europe was at rest and quiet, in chains, at the feet of the despots, would they rest? No! The same confederacy which had put down the nations and people of Europe, would immediately turn towards America, to punish us, the instigators, the first to lift up before the world the standard of republicanism. They would certainly come, flushed with victory, to pay us a visit. . . .

Ought not subscriptions be opened and an American legion now be organized, of five or ten thousand men, to cross the Atlantic, and aid in the approaching struggle of free republican government against unmitigated despotism? . . . For such a purpose, we would not hesitate to put down, at the head of one of the lists, a thousand dollars, at least, to aid our republican brethren of the old world in defending and maintaining the common cause of republican liberty. [June 8, 1849]

The tide of conquest, bearing civilization on its bosom, has ever flowed from east to west. . . . The same nation that formed the western boundary of Europe, and sent back its redundant force to the Far East, supplied the predominant element for the extension of civilization over the New World. The red men fell before the Eastern race, and followed the setting sun. From that hour the current of migration is still westward, and conquest and civilization follow in its train. Not only are the Indians driven onward to the Far West, but the subjugation of the half Indian half Spanish races of Mexico, California, the western boundary of this continent, has been attained in a single giant stride. Nor will it satisfy the young eagle to gird the Western World. He is already taking wing still westward over the Pacific ocean, and will continue his flight till the West meets the East, and the treasures of India and China, but chiefly of Japan, are poured into the lap of this republic, which will give in return the principles of liberty and civilization to the remote nations of Asia, the largest and most venerable quarter of the globe—the ancient birth-place of the human race—the origin of kingdoms, and empires, and governments. Thus the light of religion, literature and science, the arts and manufactures, and commerce, shall have circled the globe—following the sun from the east, and pursuing him westward in his track, till they have reached the east again, and have arrived at the point from which they started. This is the great law of humanity, and it is as vain to endeavor to arrest or divert it, as it is to attempt to change the electric current that passes through the earth, or the great currents of the ocean that obey the laws of nature.

Instead, therefore, of rushing now into a mad conflict with Russia in Europe, the United States will one day take the bear behind, and thus dispatch him, should he not fall in the meantime before the resistance of the principles of popular liberty. Russia moves on from the East and is preparing to overrun all Europe; but the force of the intellect and the enthusiasm for freedom may not only check that gigantic power in its career, but crush it to the earth. The course of America is clear: she will not go to Europe to attack Russia or any other nation, though always ready to repel attack made upon herself. Her destiny is onward, according to the prophetic line of Bishop Berkley—

"Westward the star of empire takes its way." [May 25, 1852]

It is well, before our sympathies take root on the Eastern question, with any side, that we endeavor to ascertain whether we have not some more direct and immediate interest in the pending European combinations, than that which we feel as common lovers of liberty and enemies of despotism. We believe that the United States are, in point of fact, as directly concerned in watching and if need be, in intervening in the progress of affairs in Europe as any nation on that continent. Not from any stake in the fate of Turkey, which may perish or thrive without affecting us in any way; but simply because the power which is now being arrayed against the projects of the Czar may tomorrow be wielded against us. . . . They [England and France] intend, after having settled the affairs of the East to their satisfaction, to turn their attention to Cuba, and to make use of their alliance to prevent the accomplishment of any scheme by which that island might fall into our hands. The evidence of this intention is too clear to admit of dispute.

What steps it may be due to our national credit to adopt in order to banish the notion of any such conspiracy from the minds of the French Emperor and his English allies, is matter for future discussion. For the present, the discovery ought at least to suggest a fresh examination of the Eastern question. If England and France openly own to a design of impertinent interference in the affairs of this continent, the presumption is that they are acting on the same unwarrantable principle in the East.

If we separate the Eastern question from the treaties and the *ultimata*, and the protocols, and the hundred petty disputes which have arisen incidentally in the course of the controversy, it will be found to be neither more nor less than a religious quarrel. The hereditary feud between the worshipper of Christ and the follower of Mahomet is at the bottom of the whole. . . . And the war that is growing out of this collision is like those between the Crusaders and the Saracens and Moors, simply a contest between Christianity and Moslemism, civilization and superstition.

It is on the side of the latter that England and France are found. These two Christian nations are seen on this momentous occasion, embracing the cause of Mohamedanism and superstition, and laboring sturdily to prevent the flow of Christianity and civilization into Turkey. If they succeed the cause of human progress may be delayed for centuries.

Is it fitting that we should follow their example, and allow a jealous animosity against a single man to delude us into a course so inconsistent with our mission among nations? And can we not, if we are satisfied that the cause of civilization is the cause of the Greek Church, discover some means of evincing our real feelings in a practical manner? [February 28, 1854]

The Russians seem to imagine that they have only to bide their time, and then halloo across the water to the United States—and that we shall jump at the prospect of an alliance against England and France, or at least, against England. This is a very bold theory. While the late Crimean war lasted, there were persons in this country who sympathized with Russia. Some from inherent dislike of England, the feeling being of the same kind as that which prompts brothers to fight and quarrel. Some from a feeling that the Western powers were really hindering the work of civilization by driving Russia from Constantinople, while they pretended to be fighting the battle of civilization against barbarism. Some from personal experience of British hauteur and incivility, of Russian courtesy. Some from a fear that if Great Britain overcame Russia, she would probably molest the United States. And a good many—these the noisiest—from connection with a class of British ex-subjects whose hatred of England is their usual stock in trade. From these reasons, the question being an open one, a great many persons living in this country, and looking at the conflict from a calm, contemplative distance, desired to see Russia the victor in the war. But to infer from this fact that the United States are ready to join Russia in any future war with England, is not warrantable. In the first place, if a census of opinion were taken throughout the United States, no doubt more friends of England would be found than enemies. And secondly, the sympathy expressed for Russia by her friends was a very cool calm business: entered into because the question was known to be purely speculative. If it ever became a real living question, then philo-Russians would think twice before they took sides. Our interests are naturally wound up with the nations which buy from us, sell to us, trade with us; which think as we do, read the same books, enjoy the same luxuries, judge by the same standards; and whatever little bickerings there may be between us, it is a great mistake to suppose that we are going to quarrel with friends like England and France, to oblige a semi-Oriental despot like the Czar, of whom we know next to nothing, and for whom we care less. [November 21, 1856]

16 THE FINAL BATTLE WITH RUSSIAN DESPOTISM

Henry Winter Davis (1817–1865)

Although born on a plantation in the South, Henry Winter Davis was a steadfast enemy of slavery. After establishing himself as an outstanding lawyer, he entered politics. A radical congressman from the border state of Maryland, he exercised considerable influence in support of the Union and on the emancipation issue. Davis was said to have been of an independent, high-minded, and uncompromising nature.

Among his many deeply held convictions was the inevitability of a final showdown between Russia and the United States, a thesis he developed in his only book, published in 1852, *The War of Ormuzd and Ahriman in the Nineteenth Century*, from which the following excerpts have been selected.[89] His choice for the title of his book of these two figures from the religion of Zoroaster—Ormuzd, the leader of the gods of good, and Ahriman, the leader of the gods of evil—reveals Davis's views of the United States and Russia.

In 1835 Tocqueville had made his well-known prediction that Russia and the United States would become the leaders in their respective hemispheres. For Davis, however, there was no doubt that the Russians would not be satisfied with half the globe, but would try for universal dominion. In this endeavor Russia would clash with the United States, the sole impediment to her world rule. Davis saw a mortal threat to his country in Russian strength in the Pacific area, her foothold on the western shores of the American continent, and her possible predominance in Europe.

WITHIN THE FOUR score years of the life of man two powers have grown from insignificance to be the arbiters of the world.

They occupy opposite continents. They are actuated by hostile principles. They are organized on antagonist theories of political power. In each is the principle of its existence absolute, pervading every department of government, infused into every element of society, and controlling the administration of affairs. There is no formally organized opposition to the existing order of things. There is no serious division of feeling or of opinion among the citizens. The people are equally devoted to the form and to the substance of their respective institutions. The foundations of both governments firmly rest on the express or implied assent of the people—who are ready to signalize their devotion on the field of battle.

Each is the incarnation of one of the great spirits, pure, absolute, unchecked, uncontrolled, unlimited, which have always striven and now strive on the theatre of nations for the mastery of mankind. These two spirits are Liberty and Despotism—the Ormuzd and Ahriman of the political world. Their purest incarnations are—The Republic of America and The Empire of Russia.

There are other free States beside those of America. There are other despotisms beside that of Russia. But there are none of either class so purely and simply the impersonations of the antagonist spirits. . . .

It is only in the Republic of America that the people, imbued with the spirit of liberty, are the recognized, uncontrolled, unquestioned souvereign power.

It is only in Russia that the Emperor is met by the cheerful, unquestioning, submissive and affectionate devotion of the people. They worship in his person the embodied souvereignty of the nation; and in the tempest of an insurrection his simple words to his children have sufficed to calm them. . . .

The progress of each power has been equally rapid and equally illustrative of the spirit and principles which animate their policy. The one has thriven amid the arts of peace and industry. The other has gorged its greatness by the spoils of war and the fruits of intrigue. . . .

Russia at this moment dictates the law to Europe from the Ural to the Bay of Biscay.

Her power is more permanent and stable in its foundations than that of either of the preceding aspirants for national dominion. . . .

The empire of Russia occupies the northern and eastern extremities of Europe. Eternal snow and ice are the unassailable bulwarks of its rear. Its eastern flank skirts far and wide into the dim confines of Asia—free from the chances of assault, and prolific in the materials for the best cavalry in the world. Its vast plains slope to the south, and tend to precipitate the mass of the empire on the fated walls of Constantinople. On the west alone is it assailable and there only during three months of the year. Retreat can hide disaster behind inaccessible snows till the favorable moment summons new armies to activity. They march to soft and many climes, allured by the splendors of art and the luxuries of civilization, where no month can numb their frames enured to the ices of the pole, and the campaign and the year are conterminous.

. . . it is not rash to say, that the centre of gravity of Europe has passed north of the Vistula: and St. Petersburg has become—the Capital of Europe.

This is what now exists over all the north of Europe, and which threatens to be universal—if it be not arrested. It is the first stage of universal empire; and, for all the purposes of aggressive ambition, it is as pregnant with danger to the independence of nations.

The power of Russia is the most dangerous at this stage—because her dominion rests on the interests of the governments she controls: and their interests are hostile to the spirit of freedom and the advance of popular government.

. . . It is animated by one spirit and policy. Its great object is the extinction of liberty in the world: and on this is founded its claim and its hope of universal empire. . . .

That the quiet reign of despotism in Europe is incompatible with liberty here has been demonstrated. That every motive of self-pres-ervation forces the despotic powers to assail us in self-defence is plain. That the concentration of the power of Europe for external aggression in the hands of one despotic dictator must seriously menace our peace and safety, and in the hands of Russia that it would be directed to that end, is only the teaching of the history of our own day: and that contingency is sufficiently near to fix the anxious eye of every statesman.

The subjection of Europe permanently to any one power would be an event of serious import to this country. It would be the creation of a power military and naval before which our utmost strength would be as nothing. Our safety would be dependent on its mercy or its justice.

Still, the most serious consideration is not—the union of Europe under one power. It is the nature of that subjection—the spirit which activates it—the purposes which it avows or pursues—and the power which shall grasp that dictatorship.

In the hands of Russia, with all its energies bent on the extermination of the intractable spirit of liberty, and the founding of a perpetual and universal despotism, such a power must menace the liberties, the safety, the very existence of this government. . . .

Russia is an *American power*—the jealous neighbor of this Republic—as insolent, aggressive, and tenacious as she has always proved herself in the opposite continent.

We cannot escape the conflict by turning our attention westward, and, abandoning Europe to her dictation, indemnify ourselves by engrossing the commerce of eastern Asia. We do not escape, but directly encounter her universal and engrossing ambition.

From her Asiatic possessions, from the Kurile and Aleutian Islands, she overlooks the natural and necessary course of our Asiatic trade—now by the occupation of California grown to stupendous magnitude, and soon destined to equal that of the Atlantic states. Her naval stations can command effectually the whole intercourse of California and Oregon with the chief seats of Chinese commerce, and render our communications unsecure at any moment. She can transfer troops and munitions of war to the coast of Oregon more rapidly than we can from the Atlantic seaboard. She is a military power in direct contact with China; and her influence can stir up the Mongol tribes, and pour them like a hail storm on the feeble and effeminate Celestials. She can now in a great measure balance the influence of

England at Pekin; her emissaries speak with almost as much authority there as at Constantinople; and a few years must give her the decided predominance.—How that control would bear on our commerce with that empire in the events which have been indicated, it takes no prophet to foretell. We should be excluded from those markets, or subjected to burthens which would strip off the profits, impede the activity, and finally destroy our Chinese trade—or we should be forced to maintain our position against Russian armies, on the spot, across the tracks of Russian navies, and at an expense and sacrifice which the most lucrative returns would scarcely compensate.

Our interests are as directly opposed as our institutions, policy, and principles. Russia is the great wheat country of Europe. To her belong the plains of the Vistula and the vast fields which pour their produce into the lap of Odessa. From these two sources come nearly all the wheat which competes with ours in the European market. She is not a manufacturing power and shews no signs of becoming such. Her whole population are divided between the plough and the sword: and to cut off or to cripple the commerce of the United States, is to rid herself of her chief, and only dangerous competitor.

Her interest, her ambition, her hate, the principles of her Czar, the proud hope of taming Europe to the yoke of absolute power, all combine to impel her into active hostility against this republic. Her territorial possessions, the conditions of our neighbors, the relations of our own territory, all afford the utmost facilities not merely for annoyance, but for injury, serious and abiding. She only waits the auspicious solution of the European problem, to seize the first invitation of internal discord or foreign embarrassment, to begin the plot that is to end with our ruin. Her peaceful and friendly tone is politic—but hollow. She would encounter one enemy at a time. She avoids sedulously the roused and combined wrath of the two great free powers of the earth [England and France]: and she willingly postpones the assault till the blow can be fatal, and securely dealt. If she triumphs in Europe, not many years will roll along ere we shall feel the influence of her diplomacy, and be called on to encounter her arms. In ordinary war she is invulnerable to us,—while we are exposed at a thousand points. She can cut off our commerce and fritter away our resources—exempted by her position from the evils of retaliation. She encounters only half the risks of war—holding in her hands the chances of success in attack, the certainty of safe and unassailable asylum in retreat after discomfiture. Like some robber knight, she pounces from her den on the honest and exposed way-farer, and retreats in safety to her hold ere the arm of vengeance can overtake her.

It is, then, the part of wisdom and foresight, for the free nations of the world—the only two whose towers still lift themselves above the flood—to see and provide against these threatening calamities now, while they are yet at a distance and allies are left, rather than to meet them singly after a few years of treacherous peace bearing all the fruits of the most disastrous war. . . .

We must be ready to make costly sacrifices of blood and treasure. Despotism will deliver terrible battle ere it loose its grip on the neck of man: and the next battle will be the final and decisive one. It will be no passing cloud; but neither sun nor stars shall appear for many days after its fury bursts over the world: and they who love fair weather and smooth seas should pray that that day be put far from them.

17 CHRISTIANITY'S TRIUMPH BY THE SWORD OF RUSSIA

Southern Literary Messenger, Richmond

The *Southern Literary Messenger*, founded in 1834, was a good periodical with regional appeal. During part of its existence it was edited by Edgar Allan Poe, who made important contributions to its pages. In questions of domestic politics the *Messenger* was, of course, partial to the South. When looking at the foreign scene, it betrayed the preconceptions and prejudices prevailing in its day. This becomes obvious in the following article on "The Destiny of Russia," which it published anonymously in 1853.[90] The Anglo-Saxon race, the protagonist of Christian civilization in the west, was expected to rule at least half the earth. Its eastern protagonist, Russia, about to attempt to subdue Turkey in the Crimean War, was to conquer the rest of the world for Christianity, the high point of civilization. That this world-wide triumph of Christianity should come by fire and sword was apparently not judged to be detrimental to its teachings.

• ———————————————————— •

HISTORY HAS incontestibly proved that for permanent stability and long-continued existence in a nation, a solid foundation and gradual rise, are absolutely necessary; and that Russia, beyond all others, has fulfilled the requirements of this immutable law; hence, even should the empire remain as it is, without further increase, it must continue long after the other nations of Europe have returned to primitive barbarism, or till the end of time. Russia has been shown

118

to be, not only the most powerful nation now on the globe, but perhaps, that ever existed: it is possessed of an inexhaustible mine of men, money and natural resources; and, above all, is founded on a spirit of devotion in its inhabitants, never equalled in the history of the race. It is situated between, and extends far into two continents, so that it may strike at pleasure upon both or either. The one continent, for many ages, has been filled with a weak and imbecile population, whom it can scatter and destroy in a moment; the other, by nations, either nerveless and ruined, or rapidly becoming so—the mere wrecks of their former greatness. With all this spread out to view, who can fail to trace the path of Russian destiny? The subjugation of Asia, from the Dardanelles to the mouth of the Ganges, from Kamschatka to the Persian Gulf, will be the first task, and will be speedily accomplished: before another half century has rolled away, the whole of that vast continent, comprising the fairest portion of the earth—the cradle of arts, the scene of the advent, the death and resurrection of the son of God, will be overrun and conquered by its iron armies. Turning from the conquest of Asia, the disciplined millions will pour down with renewed vigor upon defence-less Europe—those shadows of kingdoms passed away—and the Eastern hemisphere will bow to the supremacy of Russia.

But there are other and far deeper causes than these, at work: there are moral causes working deep at the main-spring of human affairs, which are hurrying on these great events with a more unerring certainty. We are taught by the Bible, that before the end of time shall finally come, Christianity must universally reign; must cover the entire world. No one can doubt that thousands of years must intervene before Christianity, through the common course of events, becomes predominant in Asia or Africa. It is plain, their conquest by Russia will establish the Christian religion in both these continents, in immense regions now sunk in pagan darkness, although it will be established by the sword. The question then arises, will it not seem better, more consonant with the mercy of God, that Christianity be carried to these benighted regions, even by the sword, than that they be suffered to linger on for thousands of years in heathenism? Wherever the sword of Russia falls, the religion of Christ, abused perhaps, but nevertheless, the germ will spring up in its path. There can be no alternative; Christianity must become universal by the arm of Russia, or it must, in many places, still be unknown for countless ages. There is, however, yet another cause at work, which has fixed Russia as the instrument for the final establishment of the Christian religion. However we may hurry on through life, regardless of the changes around us; however we may lay the syrens' song to our soul, the sober thinker, when he pauses, must see that all things are now indicating the fulness of time—that the human race has nearly arrived at its goal. In the enlightened portions of the globe, civilization has reached its ultimatum. A few more steps, and mankind would spurn the mortal coil Deity has set upon them, and mount to the regions of the gods; and hence they can go no further. God has fixed a limit for human progress, saying, "thus far shalt thou go and no farther": and that limit will be found in the civilization of the nineteenth century. Civilization rose immediately from the Deluge, and reached its climax in the learning of Egypt, and then disappeared. It was again revived by Greece and Rome, attained a still higher point of perfection, then sank with the Western Empire. Once more it has arisen from the darkness of the Middle Ages, in the present century, to the highest point humanity can grasp—and the end is near at hand. When civilization revived in Greece and in the Middle Ages, the world was comparatively new and its inhabitants few, and there were vast and then unknown regions to be filled up; to accomplish which, progress was still required. This is no longer the case. With the single exception of the American wilds, the world is nearly full: when they become settled, as they shortly must, there will not be a spot of unsettled earth remaining to be peopled; and the mission of mankind will be finished. There will be nothing beyond. Hitherto, almost boundless regions have ever been open for the expansion and progress of man: but this can then no longer be; for he will be spread over every portion of the entire globe: and, God has so formed human nature, that he will not permit it long to remain chafing in its bounds, after the final barrier has been reached. But it is the decree of the Almighty, that Christianity shall universally prevail before the end of time. Countless ages must elapse before the usual course of events will bring it about; and if the fulness of time is already at hand, there is, then, no alternative which we can see, save that it must come to pass through the instrumentality of Russian arms. The conquest of the East by Russia will, in all probability, fulfil another prophecy of the Bible; it will destroy the Moslem dominion, and reestablish in Palestine the wandering tribes of Israel. Thus all things, all causes, both human and Divine, seem working together for the same great end—the speedy supremacy of the Christian religion and the establishment of Russian dominion throughout the Eastern hemisphere.

It may be objected, that the United States, changing front as it is from the Atlantic to the Pacific ocean, will soon be closely connected with China, and will interrupt and check there the progress of Russia. We think this cannot be: the United States are separated by a wide ocean from China, while the situation of Russia must give it complete control whenever a Czar worthy of his position ascends the throne; and it will be remembered that not only the nearest portions of Asia to America, but part of America itself, belong to this very Russian empire. Yet, though the United States cannot check the march of Russia, it will, in all probability, as inevitably extend its domain over a hemisphere. The republican institutions may possibly change: but, whether under a republican or monarchical government, the sceptre of the American Continent from ocean to ocean, and from pole to pole, at no distant period, will be swayed by the Anglo-Saxon race; and the world will be divided into two immense empires. What then? Here we must pause—speculation itself can go no further—the problem becomes too great for other than Deity to solve.

CHARGE OF RUSSIAN CAVALRY AGAINST TURCOMANS

18 MORE SWINGS OF THE PENDULUM

New York Herald

It was *Realpolitik*, pure and simple, that guided American attitude toward Russia during the critical years of the Civil War and the Alaska Purchase. At least that is the impression to be gained from reading the editorials of the *New York Herald* during those years, our next selections.

In 1861, when the slavery issue was coming to a climax in the United States, Russia emancipated her serfs. Thus, there seemed to exist good grounds for Northerners to sympathize with Russia. Russia's own sympathies toward the cause of the North appeared to find expression in the sudden arrival of a Russian fleet in the New York harbor in 1863. Whatever the reasons for this move on the part of Russia, historians now consider it less a manifestation of goodwill toward the warring North than a flight before the threatening, superior navies of England and France. In any event, the Russian sailors were feted as friends.

During the last months of 1863, when Union victory seemed to be assured, American opinion changed abruptly and now favored the Western European nations, whose industrial resources were badly needed for reconstruction. Far-off Russia could be of little help to the shattered economy of the United States. "Barbarians they are and barbarians they will remain for some time to come, and we must say we have had enough of them," exclaimed the *Herald* on November 18, 1863, when the so-called Russian festivities, the celebrations in honor of the Russian navy, had ended.

This change of attitude was paralleled in 1867, when Russia sold Alaska to the United States. On January 15 of that year the *Herald* had still issued warnings against Russia's movement toward the Mediterranean. But in April, it hailed the *entente cordiale* between the two countries and accepted Russia's designs on Constantinople and the Bosporus. A few months later, however, Alaska was merely "a cold bite," thrown to the United States because the territory was outside vital Russian interests.[91]

•————————————————————•

ALTHOUGH THE SYSTEMS of government in the two countries are entirely different, yet there are many striking points of similarity between the United States and Russia. Both nations are comparatively young. Civilization practically began in this country with the settlement in Virginia in 1607, in New York in 1614, and in New England in 1620. Russia was an empire of barbarians until the advent of that wonderful genius, Peter the Great, in 1682. From these epochs the progress of America and Russia may be dated. The one a republic, the other a despotism, it is not a little singular that these two nations should now be firmly united by sympathy against nearly all the rest of the world, and that they should be no less firmly united in their manifest destiny in the future.

Napoleon's prophecy that Europe would be either Cossack or republican in fifty years may be verified before 1870; but this prophecy may be improved upon in the light of recent events. It is now evident that the world will be divided between the Cossacks and the republicans within the next half century. Russia is to the Eastern continent what the United States is to the Western continent—the leaven which leaveneth the whole lump. Great wars are imminent upon both continents, and when these wars are concluded the map of the world will be entirely rearranged. Russia and America will have the same enemies to fight, and we do not doubt that they will achieve the same success. Our rebellion has so completely developed the hostility of England, France and Spain towards this republic that a war with these three Powers at the conclusion of our civil war seems to be inevitable. The revolution in Poland, fomented and encouraged by France and England, has given Russia the same causes of complaint against those nations. The invasion of Mexico by France, the seizure of St. Domingo by Spain, the approval of these proceedings by England, and the assistance rendered by England and France to the Southern rebels, are the counts of our indictment against these treacherous and hypocritical neutrals. Russia charges that the Polish rebellion was incited by France and armed by England, and that it would have been suppressed long ago but for the aid of those two Powers. We do not compare the Southern rebellion with that of Poland. Such a comparison would do our rebels too much honor. But it is clear that the European governments have committed the unpardonable offence of supporting both rebellions by material aid and diplomatic endorsement, and that this offence will be punished by the great nations thus outraged and insulted.

Russia owes much of her advancement in the arts of peace and the appliances of war to the United States. We, in turn, are indebted to Russia for her cordial recognition of our enterprise and her warm sympathy in our national troubles. When the jealous English refused to allow the Russian commissioners to make copies of plans of various improvements in naval architecture, the Americans not only offered plans and specifications, but also sent models to the Russian government. The railroads, telegraphs and many of the manufactories of Russia are the result of her patronage of American talent. The earthworks with which Todleben made his magnificent defence of Sebastopol were suggested by the works erected by our revolutionary generals. Our iron-clad vessels and our new system of harbor defences will soon be adopted by our Northern ally. Every valuable improvement and invention devised by our genius is reported to Russia by her agents and is turned to her advantage. While we are steadily pushing our way to the West, Russia is advancing eastward. Our pacific telegraph across an almost uninhabited desert is paralleled by the Russian line across Siberia. The progress of the two countries continues with almost equal steps. Nor are the internal resources of Russia and America dissimilar. We are self-sustaining, and so is Russia. We are one of the great granaries of the world, and Russia is the other. We can easily place a million of soldiers in the field, and Russia is the only other nation which can accomplish anything like this stupendous feat. Forced to encounter these twin giants, the European powers will have but a slight chance of success. Such a contest, although hopeless, seems to be now impending. Our Monroe doctrine, so far from being abrogated, as Europeans assert, is solely transgressed by France and Spain; and will soon be reasserted with practical examples. Napoleon might as well attempt to destroy the Ten Commandments by telling a lie or picking a pocket as to abrogate the Monroe doctrine by invading Mexico. Behind the Ten Commandments is divinity, and behind the Monroe doctrine are the American people.

If Russia equally resents and punishes the interference of Europe in the affairs of Poland, she may be the mistress of the Old World, as we shall be of the New; and then, perhaps in a hundred years hence, these two immense Powers may meet upon the Pacific Ocean and, differing upon some question of the possession of Australia or New Zealand, may enter upon the Titanic contest which will forever decide the destinies of mankind. [August 31, 1863]

At last we can announce the close of the Russian *fetes*, or farces. Glad as we are that all the fuss and parade is over, we cannot allow the occasion to pass without a few sensible words in regard to those who have made themselves so entirely ridiculous during these farcial performances. The great Napoleon, when confined upon the island of St. Helena, uttered the memorable proverb that if you scratch a Russian you will find a Tartar beneath. Napoleon never said anything more true, and we have found it so during our recent experience in entertaining the officers of the Russian fleet now in our harbour.

We are a young nation, and we display a great deal more youthful enthusiasm than manly common sense in our hospitality toward foreigners. Trollope, Dickens, Captain Marryat, Bull Run Russell and half a hundred European scribblers have been received here with the utmost possible kindness, which they have returned by slandering, caricaturing, and abusing us as soon as they again set foot upon their native soil. Mortified as we have been by the conduct of these ingrates, we have not yet had sense enough to avoid giving opportunities for similar sneers. We entertained the Japanese princes, or bootblacks—we are not certain which they were—in a truly royal style, and they have retaliated by murdering all Americans on sight. When the Prince of Wales landed here we astonished that young man and his noble attendants by a welcome which extended from one end of the country to the other, and in which all classes and conditions of our people heartily joined. The English have rather astonished us with the manner in which they have reciprocated our attentions by supplying the rebels with a navy, offering us cannon balls for our *soirees dansantes*, and burning our merchant vessels as a response to our torchlight processions and illuminations. But why go over the old, familiar story? Suffice it to say that we have now capped the climax of absurdity by *feting* a lot of Russians who neither care for nor appreciate our hospitality, and who laugh in their sleeves at our juvenile and gushing simplicity.

Upon the arrival of the Russian fleet in our harbor we were seized with a Russian mania. Our citizen soldiers paraded the streets, muddied their trowsers, to show themselves to the Russians, and were quietly ignored at the Russian dinner. The dinner was gotten up lavishly—although lard, and tallow, and train oil would have done as well as game, and pastry and champagne—but the speeches were exceedingly farcial, especially in those portions which essayed to draw a comparison between the Emperor Alexander and President Lincoln. Then came the ball, which was, as we predicted, a farce and a failure. So ends the history of the Russian festivities; and what have we gained by them? We had that before, in a diplomatic way, and it really amounts to nothing. Russia sends her navy here to keep it safe in the event of a war with France; but we doubt if she would send it here if we needed it to aid us in fighting England. Her navy, in fact, is not worth the sending. One of our Ironsides could blow it out of water, with all the barbarians on board, in a couple of hours. How else can Russian sympathy avail us? What assistance is her barbarian legation or her barbarian diplomacy to a people able to take care of themselves? If she has any sympathy to spare let her expend it upon the Poles who have groaned for half a century under her iron yoke, and have been deprived of all her natural and national rights, except the right of being sent to Siberia. For free America to become cheek by jowl with such a despotism is contrary to all the tradition, all the sentiments and all the principles of this republic. We may have forgotten this during our recent excitement. Let us remember it now. Neither does it at all alter the case that we are contending with a rebellion, and that Russia is in the same predicament. The saying that misery loves company is not applicable to our situation. Our rebellion is the attempt of a few ambitious politicians to destroy the government in order to retain power. The Polish rebellion is the struggle of a brave people for that right of self-government of which they have been robbed. There is no coincidence, no similarity, between the two rebellions, any more than between the two governments against which the rebellions are contending. . . . We want no sympathy from Russia, no sympathy from France, no sympathy from England, no sympathy from any European government. We shall settle our difficulties for ourselves and in our own time and way; and our tremendous display of military and naval strength, and our unparalleled resources, and our unanimity of national feeling, will compel the respect and fear of the world. The genius of Liberty and of America is supremely ridiculous when she appears at a ball, and trips about on her toes like a ballet girl, in order to obtain a little worthless applause from foreigners, who are far more likely to laugh and jeer than to fall in love with her. Let her preserve her dignity, and rely upon her iron-clads and her armies, and both Russian barbarians and European neutrals will be happy to esteem and admire her. [November 12, 1863]

Russia and America, the young giants respectively of the Old and New Worlds, in whom are concentrated greater vitality and strength than in any other of the modern Powers, are at this moment, although in most respects the antipodes of each other, engaged in the same work—that of expansion and progression. They stand now upon the two continents, the one the impersonation of absolutism, the other of republicanism. No two nations at once bear a more forcible resemblance and exhibit a more striking contrast, and at this moment not two, despite the aggressive policy of Prussia or the menacing silence of France, are watched with more solicitude or are likely to accomplish more stupendous results. The specific ultimate object at which Russia aims is the acquisition of the European possessions of the Sultan. With the proud city of Constantinople, the command of the Bosporus and the commerce of the Black Sea under her control—an unbroken territory extending from the Arctic to the Mediterranean, and stretching across Asia—she would be effectually mistress of Europe. The United States do not define their aspirations, but look quietly forward to the time when the "whole boundless continent" will form one unbroken republic. The remarkable *entente cordiale*, which for a quarter of a century has been increasing between us, renders this similarity of object the more natural.

Russia and the United States must ever be friendly, the colossi having neither territorial nor maritime jealousies to excite the one against the other. The interests of both demand that they should go hand in hand in their march to empire. [April 29, 1867]

19 A SINGULAR COMPOUND OF LAZINESS AND ACTIVITY, CARELESSNESS AND GOOD NATURE

Eugene Schuyler (1840–1890)

Eugene Schuyler was one American diplomat in Russia who knew the language well, got to know the country, and studied its history. In fact, he is remembered as a scholar as well as a diplomat. After graduating from Yale and Columbia Law School, Schuyler practiced law in New York. His diplomatic career started with his appointment in 1866 to the post of U.S. consul in Moscow. In 1869 he was stationed in St. Petersburg as secretary of the legation, where he remained until 1876, acting at times as chargé d'affaires. In 1876 he was transferred to Constantinople as consul general and secretary of the legation. His reports on the Turkish massacres in Bulgaria, along with the reports of his friend Januarius Aloysius MacGahan,[92] were largely responsible for the decision of the British government not to intervene in the Russo-Turkish War of 1877–1878. These same reports resulted in the charge that he was partial to the Russians and brought about his recall. His extensive travels led to his book *Turkestan*, which was critical of Russian adventures in Asia. He translated Turgenev's *Fathers and Sons* and Tolstoy's *Cossacks*. In 1884, his most ambitious work, *Peter the Great*, was published. The selection that follows, is from an article by Schuyler of 1869.[93]

THE RUSSIAN PEASANT is a singular compound of laziness, activity, carelessness, and good-nature. When he chooses to work, he will work well and with a will, but he must be allowed his own ways, and frequent breathing-spells. He seems to have no sense whatever of the value of time, and finds it difficult to comprehend how new methods can be better than the old, or machines than hard labor. At first he will break and put out of order all the agricultural machines, not from ill will, or entirely from stupidity, but from his natural carelessness and his dislike to new-fangled notions. When he is once accustomed to them he will treat them carefully and even invent methods of repairing them. I have seen a peasant near Voronezh who was as proud of the new patent plough which he was using as he was of his horses. The climate demands more work to satisfy his necessary wants than elsewhere. But for luxuries he has little desire, and when he has worked enough to supply himself with fuel and food for the winter he stops. The innumerable festivals allowed by the church are a great temptation and obstacle to him. Beside Sundays there are forty-three fasts and festivals—non-working days, when even the manufactories and government offices are closed. Then there are fifty-six lesser holidays, on which the people are apt to be idle; and ten to one the peasant is good for nothing on the day after a holiday, as he has probably been royally drunk the day before. I remember once asking a boy how many holidays there were in the year: "They do say," he replied, "that there are only two days that are not holidays." The peasant is shrewd, makes a good bargain, loses few opportunities to make or save money; yet at all the same time he is singularly improvident. He allows his house and barns to go unrepaired, he neglects to keep up the stores of grain for a bad harvest, he will spend his last kopek in the drinking-house. Serfdom is probably more to blame than he himself for this. With his equals he is generally honest. He will always steal from his master, and he will lie on the slightest provocation. These two traits mark also the negro of the South. His greatest fault is drunkenness. . . . The love of liquor is a national failing, and nowhere, unless in England and

America, is the practice and habit of drunkenness so widespread. The government have at last taken the alarm, and measures are now being taken to reduce the number of places where liquor may be sold, and to raise its price. There are some other points in which not much can be said for the morality of the peasant. Chastity is a virtue which is much more esteemed than observed. In many parts of Russia there exists a practice similar to that known to English law as *usus primae noctis*; but in this case it is the father of the bridegroom and not the master who enjoys the privilege. In the villages, along the highroads and the great rivers, syphilitic diseases are very common. In Little Russia, however, in respect to chastity, no fault can be found.

Perhaps the most striking and agreeable trait of the Russian peasant is his abiding good-nature. He is almost always smiling, is ready to oblige you and on almost terms of equality with you. He will get angry and pour out a torrent of verbal abuse but he rarely turns to blows, and in the middle of his tirade will perhaps break out into a laugh and use entreaty or persuasion. When he is drunk he is never furious, but is always mild, tractable, and good-natured—even affectionate. It is impossible to be among these simple-hearted people without becoming much attached to them; and nowhere does one treat his servants so much as his equals as in Russia. They are always ready to talk, and you are amused with them; you may be angry and vexed at their slowness or seeming stupidity, but you don't doubt their willingness to assist you, and their good-nature disarms you. Their sympathy in all accidents that befall you is equally pleasing; and if you go on a journey, the very manner in which they kiss your hand and wish you a fervent "Go with God!" shows that there is something more than the mere relation of master and servant. Uncivilized as the Russian peasant may be, he is seldom brutal. The statistics of crime show a very small proportion of brutal crimes, and even cruelty to animals is not common. Indeed there is little malice in the Russian nature. He is always ready to pardon and forgive; no matter how deeply he may have been injured. Patience is one of his great characteristics. He can endure ill-usage, ill-fortune and hunger with a sort of religious stoicism, always expressing his trust in God, and saying of every accident, "Nitchevo, that is nothing." The same disregard of evil, indifference to chance, can also be seen in the young noble who stakes all his fortune on the turn of a card, or resolutely leads a forlorn hope, and to the entreaties of his friends exclaims, "Nitchevo, nitchevo." In fact the word itself is a sort of index to the Russian character.

Yet in spite of his stoicism even the Russian peasant has strong passions. If he is happy, he is very happy; if he is unhappy, he is wretched. Suicides for love are by no means uncommon in the villages. It is perhaps the strength of passion which makes holidays so necessary to him. He is willing to be kept down ever so strictly to hard work, provided only when his festival comes, he can "breathe out," as his phrase goes, to the utmost, and give himself wholly up to pleasure. The Russian nobles are noted for their politeness of manner, but courteousness is no less common among the peasants. That they rise and uncover when a superior approaches, is perhaps a relic of servitude; but when one peasant lad meets another on a country road, or when a porter in Moscow meets an acquaintance, he always takes off his cap, and in case of a good friend kisses him. There is, too, a certain amount of deference shown to women. The salutation is always "Brother" or "Sister." All this is so contrary to the careless nod or gruff greeting seen among the common people in most countries that it is one of the first things the traveler remarks in the streets.

There are yet two traits which deserve mention—one because it is not without parallel at home, and the other because it has recently been denied. These are inquisitiveness and restlessness. The peasant has still a nomad nature, which is by no means opposed to the social instinct. His attachment is more to his family than his village or immediate surroundings. He is ready at any time to move, himself, his house, or the whole village. This may be an inherited disposition, or it may be that with a landscape so flat and uniform as in Russia, and with the surroundings of one village repeating themselves about another, he does not feel the same attachment to locality as in most countries. . . .

The inquisitiveness of the Yankee, and of the Scotchman, is proverbial, but it is nothing to that of the Russian. It pervades all classes, from the noble to the peasant. The stranger whom you meet upon the road, will always begin the acquaintance with, "Where from and where to?" and will then ask all the details of your life, your family, and your business. But he himself is by no means reticent: without the slightest provocation he will tell you what his sister died of, or why his brother's wife ran away, or of the curious adventure of his uncle, to say nothing of his own intimate history. This makes traveling in Russia very amusing, and one can pick up a greater quantity of information on every topic without the trouble of asking. The Russian is essentially talkative, *bavard*, and speechmaking.

The Russian peasant is by no means stupid as he is often called. The children learn well and are bright and intelligent. One often meets with old men whose talk is entertaining and instructive. An intellectual business capacity often enables them to rise in the world. . . . The women, however, are densely stupid—a bad thing for the advocates of woman's equality, as they are here subject to the same conditions as the men. They share his labor, and have no discrimination made against them.

With small rude means the peasant can effect great results. Give him his time and his own way, and he will work wonders. . . .

The handicraft of the peasants is astonishing. To say nothing of wood-carving, and fabrics in silk, wool, and cloth of gold, you can buy at Tula pistols equal in workmanship to fine English ones, and the gold and silver filagree work is equal to that of Genoa. The *muzhik* can in twelve hours learn to manage the most complicated machines of a cotton factory without further assistance. This quickness of comprehension, combined with his restlessness causes him to change often his trade, a thing which injures the quality of Russian work. . . .

The peasant is born with a certain capacity of organization, and a tendency toward association, which render his future full of hope. The village is a communal society, and all the land is held in common and redistributed from time to time among the members, when need arises. It is governed by a *stárosta*, who is *elected* by the peasants, and is clothed by law with judicial powers. Whenever a peasant is an artisan he belongs to an *artél*, or co-operative association, which instructs him, finds him work, and provides him with lodging and a common table. . . .

The peasants are as a mass still uneducated, though progress is being made in this direction. The schools in the cities are open to the peasants, and in many villages infant-schools have been started. There are villages in which, owing to the energy and good-will of the master, nearly all the children can read and write. But such cases are, unfortunately, too rare. By a recent decree of the Holy Synod, Sunday-schools are allowed and recommended. Many have been started in the Government of Lamara, and though the education there is too exclusively religious, they will, doubtless, be productive of much good. Schools for the instruction of the soldiers now exist in all the barracks and permanent stations. The peasants in the cities are either servants (*izoostchiks*) or artisans, and their education is generally much better than that of their country brethren. The rudiments of an education are by no means uncommon among them.

A PEASANT COUPLE

VILLAGE ON A RUSSIAN ESTATE

20 IN PRAISE AND CONDEMNATION OF AUTOCRACY

Henry George (1839–1897)

Henry George was one of a number of nineteenth-century American writers who, largely self-taught, came to their profession via the printing trade. After having attended school for only a few years, he left home to try his hand at numerous occupations. Generally he met with little success, and he and his family suffered great privations. His encounter with the printed word opened the road to his real calling. The originality of his thinking established him as a major economist, an acknowledgment that the world still accords to him.

In 1871, when he was the editor of the *San Francisco Post*, Henry George had just begun to develop his own ideas. During that year he published his first pamphlet, *Our Land and Land Policy*. In the same year he published in the *Post* an enthusiastic article about the visit of the czarevitch, who was later crowned Alexander III (1881) and was to prove to be an archreactionary. In 1871 George may still have believed what he had expressed in his first public speech in 1865: that national policies should interpose no barrier to harmonious relations between nations.[94] But the *Post* article could no longer have been written by the Henry George who, in 1879, published his main work, *Progress and Poverty*. His comments of 1879 about the Nihilist movement were anything but laudatory to the Russian government. They reflected his concepts of democracy and liberty, which he had since developed. His article of 1871 on the czarevitch's visit and the one of 1879[95] constitute the next selection.

THERE IS, at first glance, something strange, almost ridiculous, in the enthusiasm with which the eldest son of the most arbitrary monarch on earth is being received in republican America. But allowing for mere curiosity and for flunkeyism, there is, beneath, a strong sentiment which is not without reason. Russia was our friend when we needed friends, and in their demonstrations in honor of Alexis, Americans are but returning the lavish hospitality with which the representatives of the United States have always been greeted in Russia.

Nor can these professions of regard between the great republic and the great empire be deemed insincere. Opposite in many things, they have still much in common. If not bound together by a mutual interest of spoliation or defense, neither have they any clashing aims. These Colossi, their firm feet planted upon continents; their rapid strides making the advance of all the world besides seem slow, are drawn together by the similarity of feeling with which each regards the vast future which opens before it.

Broad as is the domain of each no impassable barriers hem them in; rapid as is their progress, it seems yet hardly commenced. Each has a work to do; each a destiny to fulfil.

Through the pathless forests and over the virgin lands of the West, or toward the ancient centres of the human race, each in her way bears the torch of Christian civilization. One moving towards the setting and the other towards the rising sun; spanning each a hemisphere, the Far West meets the Further East, and upon opposite shores of the Pacific, their out-posts look upon each other.

So widely separate are their paths, that they are exempt from all the jealousies that vex relations of smaller and contiguous states. It would not vex the Russian to see the Great Republic count her stars from the frozen sea of the North to the great cape which looks to the Antarctic Ocean. The American will not feel any alarm when the cross is again raised above the crescent, and a prince whose sway extends further than the Roman eagle ever soared is throned in the city which Constantine founded for the capital of the world. It is well that the friendly feeling between these two great nations that, in all human probability, in the next century may, if they choose, divide the world between them, should be fostered and cemented in all honorable ways. And nothing can better assure the Russian people that the kindliness which they have always shown towards us is appreciated, than the enthusiasm with which their future ruler is greeted in his visit to the United States.

The Russian Nihilists are making a terrible fight—"An eye for an eye, and a tooth for a tooth." For every one of their number who suffers an official is sacrificed. The suddeness and mysteriousness with which the law of reprisal is carried out adds to this effect. There is evidence that it has already paralyzed the Russian police organization. It is a mistake to suppose that these Russian Nihilists belong to the poorer and more ignorant classes. Nihilism has its strength among the junior members of the aristocracy, among the students of the universities, among the officials themselves. Awakening from a long lethargy the cultivated mind of Russia aspires to greater freedom, and dreams of the grand idea of the equality and brotherhood of man, but opposed by the iron rule of a corrupt autocracy it can only show itself this way. The future of Russia is one of the most interesting problems. The leaven of the times is working, and Russian imperialism cannot long exist. And beneath the bureaucracy which now weighs upon Russia lies the best basis for true republicanism which Europe presents in the old Slavonic village communities, where the real life of the people goes on. Napoleon said Europe must be either Cossack or republican. It may be that the Cossack will yet teach Europe republicanism.

21 THE DAY OF PLEASURE FOR PEASANTS IS COMING!

Edna Dean Proctor (1829–1923)

Edna Dean Proctor was already recognized as a poet by some when she was only fourteen. After studying drawing and music, she taught school. During the Civil War her passionate verses and other writings in defense of the Union made her known throughout the United States, as did her "Song of the Ancient People," a poem about the Zuñi Indians, which was published in 1893.

Edna Dean Proctor traveled widely on the American continent as well as in Europe. A trip to Russia in 1866 inspired many poems about Russian subjects and a widely read travel book, *A Russian Journey*, published in 1872. A great admirer of Russia and the Russian people, she expected that country to become equal to her own in wealth and power. Having been an ardent abolitionist, she was especially drawn to the subject of the liberation of the serfs, which she celebrated in verse and in prose.

The first selection, from *A Russian Journey*,[96] mirrors the great hopes that emancipation of the serfs had raised in her. The second, the preface to the 1890 edition of her *Russian Journey*, shows her great disappointment on realizing that the freeing of the serfs by itself had not improved their lot. She now hoped for land reforms and, indeed, a complete change of Russia's political system, by which full emancipation of the peasants and, with it, the flowering of Russia could at last be brought about.

JUST WHERE THE TOWN met the steppe, we came upon a long line of carts from the far country, filled with wheat for the market. It was a characteristic and interesting sight, for formerly all the grain was brought to town in this way. The carts were similar to those of the Tartars, wholly of wood, without tire or nail. Each held perhaps twenty-five bushels of wheat, and was drawn by two oxen, gray, small, and slow-moving cattle, attached to it by a harness of rope. The axles would get on fire with the constant friction, were it not for frequent use of the vile grease carried in a little pot hanging beneath.

But how shall I describe the men walking by the team? Never before had I so vivid an idea of a serf. Their faces were as dull as those of the bullocks they drove, and they moved in the same lethargic way. They seemed to be rather fair of hair and complexion, but were so begrimed with dust, it was difficult to tell. Some were bareheaded, and all wore blouses and trousers of coarsest sacking, fastened about the middle with a rope or a strap of leather. Gloomily stupid, they looked as if they had never had an emotion in their lives. They had come, perhaps from the borders of Poland, perhaps from Kiëff, for then the railway thither was unfinished. We looked after them as they plodded on, and commiserated their lot. Born of ancestors equally degraded, they had nothing to wake thought or hope or ambition. The grain they carried was not their own, but belonged to some landed proprietor who would pay them a mere pittance for the journey. They had travelled ten or twelve miles a day and then halted; and while their cattle ate the grass by the roadside, they had made a meal of buckwheat porridge or rye bread,— for wheat they seldom taste,—and then slept under their carts. It was one of this class to whom Prince Demidoff refers in his account of travel through this region—a man ill, and without aid, in whose hut he sought refuge from a storm. "Ah," said this uncomplaining sufferer, when his visitor expressed pity for his condition, "peasants were not sent into this world for their own pleasure."

Thank God! the day of pleasure for peasants is coming! The Czar has made them free men, and with the knowledge of their manhood their dormant faculties will awaken. The elder men of this generation will not greatly change; but their children will have education and gain wealth and power. They will send their own wheat to Odessa, and eat of the best of the land at home, and tales of the days of servitude will seem as far off as if they had been in another world!

Twilight was deepening as we returned to the hotel. It was the "Name's day" of the Czar—the festival day of Saint Alexander Nevsky, whose name he bears,—and the principal streets and buildings were brilliantly illuminated. The Exchange presented a beautiful appearance, with a motto in Russ blazing upon its front, and, beneath, the Emperor's cipher surmounted by a crown, and encircled with flame. The harvest moon shone over the sea; the streets were filled with merry people; and, remembering the uplifting of the nation, we could have exclaimed as heartily as any Russian of them all, "Honor and long life to the Czar!"

It is more than twenty years since the journey was made of which these pages are a record. Then, in spite of fears and reactions, Russia was still flushed with joy and hope from the Emancipation of the serfs, and her friends, everywhere, believed a better day had dawned for her. Through this rosy glow I looked at the future of Czar and people.

The Emancipation of the serfs was a great and daring reform, one which will keep the name of Alexander II. forever illustrious among the Czars; but a reform so inevitable that it could not have been long delayed. Yet it was only the first step towards the goal of rounded, individual manhood to which the whole human race is tending. To pause there, was like lingering upon the chord of the seventh while the ear cries imperiously for the octave; like making foundation and crypt strong and spacious, but never rearing, thereupon, the noble cathedral with its crowning spire; nay, like staying the sun at dawn, with earth longing for the full glory of his beams.

The peasants compose by far the largest part of the population of Russia, and, with the officials, (drawn from the higher ranks,) the army, and the police, make up the nation. In order that this great body of liberated men might appreciate the blessings of freedom and of ownership of land, and be able to use them, they needed education, and the most helpful measures which the combined wisdom of the country could devise. But with such limited bounty;—their allotments of land proving small in proportion to the taxes imposed—such utterly inadequate provisions; and with their lack of self-reliance and enterprise, due to the irresponsible, careless ways of servitude; many have questioned, in their ignorance and disappointment and helplessness, whether the old days were not, after all, better than the new. Emancipation freed them from the dominion of their masters; but they are still the creatures of the Government, still almost voiceless in its councils, still hampered on every side by restrictions and penalties which nothing but mighty, concerted action on their part could enable them ever to throw off. And when it is remembered that every village is under the surveillance of the police, and that the whole force of the Empire can be employed to search out offenders and put down insurrections, the difficulty of such action, however wisely and justly attempted, will be understood. But in this age, when liberty is in the air, and the problem of government by the people and for the people has been triumphantly solved, it will be as impossible for the great Russian nation to be long held in such bondage, as it would be to keep the majestic current of the Volga prisoned in ice, and the trees upon its banks bare of leaves, when winds blow soft from the south and the sun shines on forest and stream with the warmth and splendor of June.

Of all Aryan races, the Russian Slavs, with their frankness, their simplicity, their gentle endurance, and yet their force, their imagination, their quick, intense sympathy, their unbounded power of losing themselves in a feeling, an idea; their capacity for self-sacrifice, their pliancy, their mysticism, their ardent faith,—seem to possess most of what we may fancy were the characteristics of the primitive people in the highlands of Asia. Indeed, to their patriarchal bias, their tendency to regard themselves as children and the Czar as a father who wishes them nothing but good, must in a great measure be ascribed their long submission to despotic rule; for, as between man and man, democracy and a sense of brotherhood are strong in

their blood. No just estimate of them can be made without considering that, since the dawn of their history, they have been the bulwark
of Europe against Asia. While the Western nations were free to
devote themselves to their own affairs, or to wars with their equally
civilized neighbors, Russia was invaded by hordes of fierce Pagan
and Mohammedan Mongols and Tartars, led now and again by some
of the ablest generals and administrators the world has known; her
towns pillaged and burned, her fields wasted, her inhabitants
slaughtered, or driven into slavery more cruel than death. For
centuries she was the vassal of the Khans; her Princes humble
servitors at Tartar camp and court,—obliged to journey even as far
as the Amoor to pay tribute and have the right to their principalities
confirmed. The Crescent beneath the Cross, on the domes of
Russian churches and monasteries, is to-day a conspicuous memento
of the dreadful struggle and the final victory.

This savage strife, this long oppression by such hated foes, could
not fail to deeply affect the national character,—to blend ferocity
with force, cunning and dissimulation with wisdom and prudence,
the servile ways of the Asiatic with the simple frankness of the Slav.
And when the Khans were at last overthrown, and the Russian states
consolidated into an empire, the Czars copied this despotic rule, and
made the people mere instruments of their will. But, for enlightened
men, the day of Khans and autocrats has passed, never to return. To
the fact that the Emperor will not see this, and give the people their
proper share in the government, thus securing more justice and good
faith and honesty in every branch of the administration, the terrible
events of recent years are due. And utterly misguided and insane as
some of the defenders of liberty have been, their patriotic devotion,
their heroic deaths, will not be in vain. The whole intelligent world is
hastening to be free. The ages of the future belong everywhere to the
people; and in Russia, this bitter conflict, however protracted, can
only end in their triumph.

With the approach of summer, the woods and steppes of Russia
burst into sudden green and beauty. The wind sings through the firs,
and sways the young leaves of the birches and lindens, wafting their
delicate perfume to the fields. The hum of bees fills the air. The
cooing of doves is heard in the hamlets. The grassy sea of the steppes

is bright with flowers,—scarlet poppies, yellow broom, gay tulips, brilliant cockles, purple larkspur—countless blooms that give their rich tints to the day, and exhale their fragrance with the evening dews; while the lark, soaring from the grass, and the nightingale warbling in the thicket, thrill dawn and moonlight with their delicious melody. The great plains bask in the sun, and the wind, that has stolen from the Altai and the Oural, sways the green expanse in waves of light and shade, to the far horizon. So soft! so fair! but, alas, so fleeting! Soon the flowers wither; the grass grows brown and sere. Clouds obscure the sun; mists veil the distance; the days rise chill; and while song and the sweet breath of summer seem hardly to have left the air, fierce blasts sweep down from the Pole, covering the once green and glowing sea with a pall of snow; and from the bare and gloomy thickets come the rustling of the dead leaves, the creaking of the branches, and anon the howling of the wolves as they rage in their hunger, and gather to pursue and seize the passing traveler. The Russian nature, with favorable conditions, is like forest and steppe in summer, full of peace and grace and charm; swayed by sympathy and feeling, as grass and bough by the passing breeze; inclined to believe and love and trust, even as the steppe looks up confidingly, and reflects the smile or the sadness of the sky. But it has also the strength and terror of steppe and forest; and under the winter of injustice and tyranny and cruelty, its impulses, its energies, its affections, become pitiless blasts and devouring wolves.

God grant that a radical change may come in the affairs of this great nation,—come quietly, justly, nobly; that the rights of the long-suffering people may be recognized; and that unbearable wrongs, and desperate assassinations, and Siberian horrors such as Mr. Kennan has so vividly portrayed, may no longer shock the world! And when it is Free Russia; when, under wise and liberal rule, the varied populations of this huge domain—one sixth of the earth's surface—can develop fully and naturally; when the passionate patriotism, the philosophy, the poetry, the wit of the people, are no longer repressed or exiled or hidden in dungeons; when the country's resources are more honestly applied for its advantage; when education is open to all;—what marvels may we not hope for, what inventive genius, what practical skill, what scientific discovery, what music, what art, what literature, in these mingled races dowered with the gifts of Europe and Asia,—unique capacities which as yet they have hardly begun to use!

There is an old and beautiful belief in Russia that "Mother Earth" knows the secrets of the future, and that, if one in silence lays his ear reverently to the ground and listens, the events of days to come will be revealed. O Russian Earth! art thou not weary of bringing forth children for destruction and woe, and for such despair that they yearn to be folded again in thine embrace? Make thou a compact with the Celestial Powers; and when thy sons and daughters listen at thy breast, let them no longer hear the wails borne on Siberian winds, the moans from prison cells, the lamentations, the murmurs, the awful threats, of an oppressed and outraged people, but gladden their hearts with omens of joy,—with songs and thanksgivings, and the inspiring words of Liberty and Peace!

A RUSSIAN PEASANT, OR SERF

PEASANT CABINS

22 RUSSIAN SOLDIERS

Januarius Aloysius MacGahan (1844–1878)

Januarius Aloysius MacGahan, the "greatest and noblest of the knights-errant of the press," earned his living as a bookkeeper while studying law and trying to become a reporter. In 1869 he left for Europe, became proficient in several languages, and worked as correspondent for the *New York Herald* during the Franco-Prussian War of 1870–1871. He continued as such in St. Petersburg in 1871.

In 1872 MacGahan traveled with General William Tecumseh Sherman through the Caucasus. During a stay in the Crimea he became well acquainted with the Russian court and eventually conceived a great liking for Russia. Refused permission to accompany the Russian expedition to Khiva, in what is today Soviet Uzbekistan, he traveled on his own across the Central Asian desert and witnessed in 1873 the fall of the city. After his return to Europe he published his observations under the title *Campaigning on the Oxus and the Fall of Khiva*. He followed the Russian army during the Russo-Turkish War of 1877–1878 and, along with Eugene Schuyler, was instrumental in changing British attitudes toward Turkey by publicizing Turkish atrocities in Bulgaria. The Bulgarians rewarded him with the title "Liberator." Although he died during that war, he had by then acquainted Americans with the Eastern Question, the political problems presented by the decline of the Ottoman Empire.

The following excerpts from *Campaigning on the Oxus and the Fall of Khiva*[97] contain vivid portrayals of the Russian professional officer and of the conscripted moujik soldier. Conscription was a heavy burden on the Russian people, especially the poorer classes who could not buy their freedom from military service. In 1873 the

149

term of service was still fifteen years, having been reduced in the 1860s from twenty-five years. In 1874 it was further reduced, as a rule to six years of active service and nine years in the reserves.[98]

•———————————————————————————•

ANDREI ALEXANDROVITCH is a slightly exaggerated type of the Russian officer in Turkistan—I might say of a large class of officers throughout the entire empire. They have not all been reduced to the ranks several times, and they are not all ensigns at forty; but the career of each of them is parallel to that of Andrei Alexandrovitch in every other particular. They have all been in the Guard; they have all squandered their fortunes in it; they have all followed faithfully in the beaten track of their predecessors. All are careless of the future, determined to make the most of the present; and all lead the same easy, indifferent, vagabond kind of life. They pass most of their time in playing cards; the mania of the Russians of all classes, indeed, for play is most excessive. I have seen them sit down and play for forty-eight hours, scarcely ever rising from the table during the whole time. I had thought only savages could evince such a passion for gaming; and the truth is, this passion among the Russians is a relic of barbarism, which still clings to them.

They never study; and they no more bother their heads about the future operations of the army, or even the orders for the morrow, than does one of their own soldiers. In most armies on a campaign like the present, the officers would all know and discuss the plan of operations, the movements about to be made, and what would be required for their execution. They would all have maps and all the information to be obtained regarding the route over which they were marching. . . .

It is not to be supposed from this that the Russians are poor officers. They are as brave as lions; and there is not one among them that would hesitate to lead a forlorn hope, or that would not walk up to certain death with as much coolness as to dinner. They obey orders with a kind of blind, unreasoning heroism, that is only equalled by that of their own soldiers. Generous, kindly, pleasant fellows withal, ever ready to offer you their hospitality or do you a favour, they are sure to win your affection and esteem.

The Russian officers have very strong likes and dislikes. For the Americans and the French they have feelings of the utmost friendliness. They speak, by preference, the French language; love French literature and French music; and they endeavour to imitate French ways of living. . . .

Ivan Ivanoff is a soldier in the regiment of Andrei Alexandrovitch. . . . Torn in early youth from village home and friends, to give fifteen or twenty of the best years of his life to the Tsar, he leaves all the hopes and desires of ordinary men far behind him. For twenty years he has nothing to look forward to but the routine of camp life. There are no pictures of wife and children, and pleasant fireside for him. Most of the friends of his youth he will never see again. He knows that long ere he returns to his village father and mother will be dead, sweetheart married, brothers and sisters grown old, and himself forgotten. His whole life has been changed; he has become another kind of being. Perhaps the change at first was bitter; he may have wept at it. His poor home was not very attractive and comfortable; but it was home, nevertheless, and he will never see it again. But the great machine of State soon crushed him to uniformity, and moulded him to his place. Thenceforth he has only been an animated automaton, moved by a will far above and beyond his comprehension; he has submitted blindly and unresistingly to his fate. The iron yoke is so solidly fixed that he never thinks of trying to throw it off. It is not in his character to struggle against the inexorable. God has willed it. It would be sinful as well as useless to repine, and he determines to make the best of a hard lot.

But amid the bustle and excitement of a soldier's life he loses the pensive sadness of his father, isolated in his remote far away village. He has little to hope, it is true; but then he has nothing to lose, and that is a source of unhappiness removed, and he becomes the merriest fellow in the world. . . .

Ivan Ivanoff has a confidence in the integrity and ability of his officers, which is highly commendable and edifying. He believes them to be infallible; he is sure they always do the best thing that is to be done, and in the very best way. Therefore he never mutinies. Another soldier may grumble if he have not milk for his coffee, or meat at least once a day. Ivan is far above complaining of such trifles. If no meat is given him, it is evidently because there is none. Or if the meat furnished is rotten, it is because of the hot weather, and there is no help for it. If his shoes are worthless, and his feet get frozen, it is by reason of the cold. If his biscuits are worm-eaten, it is the fault of the worms. He never thinks of blaming anybody. If by any bungling mistake he is brought under fire, where his comrades fall around him by the hundred, and his regiment undergoes sure annihilation, it is the will of God, and must be submitted to. Nor does it ever occur to him to correct the judgment of his officers by running away. In short, Ivan Ivanoff thinks, with Pope, that whatever is is right, and therefore is willing to take things as they are. He will live happily on black bread and tea, and never think of complaining.

Ivan Ivanoff has nobody to love but his comrades and his officers; and them he loves passionately, although in a stolid, unconscious sort of way. It is no uncommon thing for eight or ten soldiers to be killed in attempting to carry off a wounded comrade. There is nothing melodramatic about Ivan, either. He will make the most heroic exertions without even being aware that he is doing anything out of the way, or that merits commendation. There is a kind of unconscious heroism about Ivan that is sublime. . . .

In short, Ivan Ivanoff is the officer's ideal of the soldier; and, everything considered, is the best soldier in the world.

RUSSIAN ARMY ON THE TURCOMAN STEPPES

23 SO UNLIKE AND YET SO SIMILAR

Walt Whitman (1819–1892)

When writing to the Russian translator of his *Leaves of Grass,* Walt Whitman called attention to the dissimilarities between Russia and the United States. The political institutions of the two countries appeared to him "so unlike at first glance." As he explained in his *Democratic Vistas,* "over there," meaning Europe as a whole, he saw "belief in the necessary absoluteness of established dynastic rulership, temporal, ecclesiastical, and scholastic as furnishing the only security against chaos, crime, and ignorance." This he contrasted to the American "doctrine or theory that man, properly trained in sanest, highest freedom, may and must become a law, and a series of laws, unto himself."

Whitman put greater stress, however, on the analogies which he found in the American and Russian peoples themselves. His love of the common people, though "ungrammatical, untidy, and their sins gaunt and ill bred," did not stop with his own countrymen. In fact, his references to the Russians in the letter to his Russian translator,[99] which follows, parallel his characterization of the American people in the 1855 preface to his *Leaves of Grass*: he called America "a teeming nation of nations," a land of "hospitality which forever indicates heroes," of "roughs and beards and space and ruggedness that the soul loves." America's genius he found in the common people, "their manners speech dress friendships—the picturesque looseness of their carriage . . . their deathless attachment to freedom."

Whitman's remarks to his translator are to be acknowledged not as polite or sentimental rhetoric but as an expression of deep interest

154

in Russia and the Russians. He had been reading a great deal about the country and its peoples.[100] This interest in things Russian may have been awakened by the friendship that Russia showed to the United States during the Civil War and by the abolition of serfdom in Russia at the time when the slaves were freed in America. The efforts of the Russian revolutionaries against the "hoggish meanness, special and general, of the feudal and dynastic world over there, with its *personnel* of lords and queens and courts, so well dressed and so handsome," could not but find a sympathetic echo in Whitman. And finally, he may have been aware of the parallel that Van Wyck Brooks found,[101] between his own prophetic vistas of America's destiny and the world evangelism of the Slavophiles, between his own youthful and exuberant nationalism and the similar aspirations expressed by contemporary Russians.

Camden, New Jersey, U.S.A. Dec. 20, '81.

DEAR SIR:—Your letter asking definite endorsement to your translation of my *Leaves of Grass* into Russian is just received, and I hasten to answer it. Most warmly and willingly I consent to the translation, and waft a prayerful *God speed* to the enterprise.

You Russians and we Americans! Our countries so distant, so unlike at first glance—such a difference in social and political conditions, and our respective methods of moral and practical development the last hundred years;—and yet in certain features, and vastest ones, so resembling each other. The variety of stock-elements and tongues, to be resolutely fused in a common identity and union at all hazards—the idea, perennial through the ages, that they both have their historic and divine mission—the fervent element of manly friendship throughout the whole people, surpass'd by no other races—the grand expanse of territorial limits and boundaries—the unform'd and nebulous state of many things, not yet permanently settled, but agreed on all hands to be the preparations of an infinitely greater future—the fact that both Peoples have their independent and leading positions to hold, keep, and if necessary, fight for, against the rest of the world—the deathless aspirations of the innocent centre of each great community, so vehement, so mysterious, so abysmic—are certainly features you Russians and we Americans possess in common.

As my dearest dream is for an internationality of poems and poets, binding the lands of the earth closer than all treaties and diplomacy —as the purpose beneath the rest in my book is such hearty comradeship, for individuals to begin with, and for all the nations of the earth as a result—how happy I should be to get the hearing and emotional contact of the great Russian peoples.

To whom, now and here (addressing you for Russia and the Russians, and empowering you, should you see fit, to print the present letter, in your book, as a preface), I waft affectionate salutation from these shores, in America's name.

W. W.

24 NO NATION MORE CHARITABLE AND HUMANE

Cassius Marcellus Clay (1810–1903)

Cassius Marcellus Clay, a politician of turbulent character and career and a close friend of Abraham Lincoln, became an ardent abolitionist while studying at Yale. Because his firmly stated position on slavery was unacceptable to his fellow Kentuckians, he could not realize his political ambitions, notwithstanding his talents, family background, wealth, and colorful personality. In 1861 Lincoln appointed him minister to Russia. When the Civil War began he refused to serve in the Union army so long as the government did not take measures to abolish slavery in the states of the Confederacy. He served again as minister to Russia from 1863 to 1869.

Clay's views on the obvious class distinctions in Russia, where his social acceptance by the nobility seems to have affected his humanism, are unexpected in terms of his stand on slavery in the United States. But it is well to keep in mind that the following letter[102] was written by a Southern gentleman who had looked honestly at his own country and found much wanting.

•————————————————————•

EDITOR KENTUCKY HERALD:—In your journal of December 12th is a paper which is a type of the malignant calumnies of the anti-Russian press for a century or more. I lived in St. Petersburg for nearly nine years, and made Russian life a study; mingling with all classes for that purpose. I dined with the Emperor and imperial families, and took cabbage soup and black bread with the woodmen who came from the interior on boats and rafts. Perhaps there is no American living or dead who can speak with more authority than I can on the real character of Russia. I believe that there is no more charitable and humane nation on earth than Russia. I give the proof. There are no deaths by absolute poverty in Russia as in the great cities of Paris, London, New York, and other European cities. Besides the charitable associations established by law, the first nobles in Russia, men and women, yearly, by organized societies, collect funds by gifts, needle-work, and other methods, for clothes, soup-houses, and bread, which is distributed all winter in St. Petersburg; and such methods are pursued in other cities. The infants that are drowned and thrown into sewers in Europe and America are taken at a day old, if need be, and brought up at the public expense in St. Petersburg, Moscow, and other cities. These children, when grown up to a suitable age, are put to service, and many make a generous living. Russia liberated her slaves not by war, and gave them lands. America did neither. I dined with the nephew of Prince Dolgorouki, Governor-General of Moscow, Viceroy, and a liberated serf or slave was at the table as a guest, and made the best dinner-speech on the occasion. The Russians open all their pleasure-grounds, beside the public parks, to the whole people. They never bar the gates and close the doors against "the rabble," as in England and America. In the summer the yards are open and the windows without blinds, that the humblest peasants may see and hear the music. On all great occasions of a private nature, all the poor are feasted or otherwise entertained by suitable means. In England and America even house-servants are treated with contempt. The Russian noblemen speak kindly always to their inferiors; the English and Americans out of the South rarely ever. The Russian Empire is large and sparsely populated, so that the means of subsistence do not at all press upon the increase of population. In the large cities, as I said, no absolute suffering for the necessaries of life is possible.

Now, as to prisons. There was at no time whilst I was in Russia, so far as I know and believe, one equal in its infamy to the Kentucky Penitentiary. And Governor Blackburn deserves not denunciation, but eternal honor, for his manhood and philanthropy, against the barbarous clamors of the press, for his reform. When I was in St.

Petersburg the cholera was several times in that city of six hundred thousand and there was no more sensation than if the measles or whooping-cough prevailed. Every subject of the disease was taken at once to wholesome hospitals, well attended; and then, when convalescent, returned, without charge, to their homes. The streets of St. Petersburg were an hundred times cleaner than the streets, alleys, and back-yards of Richmond. They never burn down the pest-houses in Russia as they did the other day in Madison County, when small-pox prevailed. As to prisons and Siberia, I am glad to have an opportunity to refute some of the world-wide calumnies of the anti-Russian press. Siberia is not so vile a country as the French penal colony of Cayenne, nor the original Australia of England. Three Siberian-born ladies married nobles in St. Petersburg—one the Prince Suwarrow, the grandson of the Prince Suwarrow of Napoleon's times. The other sisters married well—one an officer on the staff of the Emperor. I have heard them speak of the "fatherland" as would a German. And these were the descendants of Siberian exiles. I do not hesitate to say that, of all the people I ever knew, the Russians are the most genial and hospitable. It is true the ranks in Russia are very distinct and marked; but the humane spirit of Russia thaws all coldness, breaks all conventional barriers, and fuses the whole into one national feeling, as in no other land. That is the reason that Russians never emigrate. That is the reason of the invincible courage of the Russian army. What calumniators call "stolidity" is unshaken and heroic patriotism. I could fill a book with similar proof, but I hold—

> "Wad but some power the giftie gie us,
> To see oursel's as ithers see us!"

C. M. Clay.

White Hall, Ky., *December* 14, 1883.

25 LONG LIVE THE RUSSIAN PEOPLE!
Robert Green Ingersoll (1833–1899)

Known as "the great agnostic," Ingersoll, a self-educated man who eventually became a lawyer, took an active part in politics and in the Civil War, during which he served as a soldier in the Union army. A famous lecturer, he attracted large audiences to whom he explained agnosticism while questioning the bases and attacking the tenets of Christianity. The unorthodoxy of his views, which contrasted with his charming manners, extended to political matters, but it did not lessen the demand for him as a public speaker.

His forceful comments on the coronation of Alexander III,[103] who in 1881 succeeded to the throne upon the assassination by nihilists of Alexander II, illustrate that his radical, iconoclastic views were not confined to American institutions. They reflect his disdain of autocracy and the disappointment of liberals about the failure of the emancipation of the serfs, whose lot was hardly improved by their freedom and who had to wait until 1906 for a meaningful land reform.

———————————————————

WHILE READING the accounts of the coronation of the Czar, of the pageants, processions, and feasts, of the pomp and parade, I could not help thinking of the poor and melancholy peasants, of the toiling, half-fed millions, of the sad and ignorant multitude, who belong body and soul to this Czar.

I thought of the backs that have been scarred by the knout, of the thousands in prison for having dared to say a whispered word for freedom, of the great multitude who have been driven like cattle along the weary roads that lead to the hell of Siberia.

The cannon at Moscow were not loud enough, nor the clang of the bell, nor the blare of the trumpets, to drown the groans of the captives.

I thought of the fathers that had been torn from wives and children for the crime of speaking like men.

And when the priests spoke of the Czar as the "God-selected man," "the God-adorned man," my blood grew warm.

When I read of the coronation of the Czarina I thought of Siberia. I thought of the girls working in the mines, hauling ore from the pits with chains about their waists; young girls, almost naked, at the mercy of brutal officials; young girls weeping and moaning their lives away because between their pure lips the word Liberty had burst into blossom.

Yet law neglects, forgets them, and crowns the Czarina. The injustice, the agony and horror in this poor world are enough to make mankind insane.

Ignorance and superstition crown independence and tyranny. Millions of money squandered for the humiliation of man, to dishonor the people.

Back of the coronation, back of all the ceremonies, back of all the hypocrisy there is nothing but a lie.

It is not true that God "selected" this Czar to rule and rob a hundred millions of human beings.

It is all an ignorant, barbaric, superstitious lie—a lie that pomp and pageant, and flaunting flags, and robed priests, and swinging censers, cannot change to truth.

Those who are not blinded by the glare and glitter at Moscow see millions of homes on which the shadows fall; see millions of weeping mothers, whose children have been stolen by the Czar; see thousands of villages without schools, millions of houses without books, millions and millions of men, women and children in whose future there is no star and whose only friend is death.

The coronation is an insult to the nineteenth century.

Long live the people of Russia!

A PART OF THE OLD TOWN OF NÍZHNI NÓVGOROD

TOBÓLSK—THE UPPER PLATEAU

A MARCHING PARTY OF EXILES
PASSING A TRAIN
OF FREIGHT-SLEDGES

CORONATION OF ALEXANDER III

26 MYSTICISM AND PESSIMISM
Edmund Noble (1853–1937)

Edmund Noble, a man deeply interested in social and political conditions of Russia and its history, emigrated to the United States from his native Glasgow when he was nineteen. He returned to Europe to edit several English newspapers and to work as the foreign editor of the *New York Herald*. In the years 1882–1884, he visited Russia twice for the London *Daily News*. From these visits dates his preoccupation with the country.

After the assassination of Alexander II in 1881, the suppression of all liberal thought and movements cast the intellectual circles of Russia into gloom. Noble's views on the melancholy character of the Russian people may be read, to some extent, as a reflection on the situation in Russia as it prevailed during his visits. His books and numerous articles on Russia deal with her social, political, and cultural aspects and her history. The following selection is an excerpt from his *Russian Revolt*, published in 1885.[104]

•————————————————————————————•

MYSTICISM, as a national trait, is produced by oppressive conditions of national life; mysticism in religion arises out of dry and lifeless formalism. Yet, in whatever guise it may present itself, mysticism is ever the result of irritation, and always assumes an attitude antithetical to authority, whether the dogmas opposed be theological or political. . . .

The conditions of Russian life in the seventeenth and eighteenth centuries had laid upon minds and hearts with so heavy a weight that the people were glad to fly for relief to the wildest dreams, to the strangest faiths, to the most fantastic illusions which highly wrought religious ingenuity could invent. The Tatar domination was long over, but a new domination had arisen, more powerful and more relentless, of wider range, of deeper humiliation. The more centralized the state became, the heavier had grown the fiscal burdens of the people; the greater the autocracy at the summit of national life, the greater the enslavement at its base. Nor was there any sufficing help for this state of things in the ministrations of the Greek Church. Minds that found it a source of light and life during the dark hours of the Mongol oppression now looked vainly for the consolation to the national faith. Its assumption to authority, its alliance with the civil power, its Byzantine elements, all prepared it for the *raskol* [schism]. But it was the dreary, lifeless formalism of its worship that sharpened the dissenter's longing for a freer and more vital spiritual activity than any that it could attain within the limits of authority and tradition.

In religious soil Russian mysticism bore abundant fruit, and is active as an element of dissent to this day. We also see it in the "men of God" of the political propagandas and conspiracies of 1873. But it was destined to occupy a still wider field. Waiting on the new culture from Europe it gave its color to some of the earliest productions of the national literature. Scarcely a single Russian writer of note is altogether free from the wider tendencies of mysticism; not a few have manifested the quality in a degree highly marked. . . .

This coincidence of the individual process with the racial and historic process is of itself evidence that neither in the one case nor in the other is the phenomenon a mere accident, but a part of the national life and a result of its conditions.

It is, at the same time, true that a complex mental condition like mysticism can only have a limited field of activity and manifestation. The tendency really universal in Russia is to pessimism. This penetrates all spheres of thought, gives its hues to every coterie and school, creates resemblances between the most diverse productions of the pen, restores as with a bond of gloom the shattered solidarity of society, and between human beings separated by impassable gulfs of rank and position stretches a connecting link of dreary dependency and common despair. Mysticism enters readily into composition with some elements; with others it is uncompromisingly irreconcilable. Pessimism goes everywhere, combines with everything. Not to be pessimistic in Russia is to be divorced from all contact and sympathy with the national life; to be cut off, either by foreign birth or by some monstrous denial of nature, from the tree of national development. All influences and epochs have contributed to the tendency. A monotonous landscape, the loss of free institutions, Byzantinism with its cruel law-giving and ascetic tyranny, the fiscal burdens of the new state, the antitheses suggested by European culture, the crushing of the individual, the elimination from Russian life of all those healthy activities which engage civilization in other countries, the harassing restrictions upon thought and movements, the state-created frivolities of society,—all these have contributed to the gloom of the mental atmosphere until to-day pessimism may be said the normal condition of all Russian thought. . . .

"Russian sadness"—*russky pechal,* as Nekrassov [a nineteenth-century poet] called it—invades all the inner life of the people. I know of no altruism more agreeable than this power which Russians have of separating themselves from the interests of their own personality, in order that they may contribute gaiety and liveliness to the general enjoyment,—this cheerful *insouciance* below which, sacrificed to the social exigencies of the moment, melancholy, sorrow, all depths of despair may lie hidden. It is this versatility which constitutes the chief charm of Russian society. But the Russian has his inner as well as his outer world, and between the two stretches a distance relatively immense. The outer is shown to strangers and acquaintances; with the inner only intimates and relatives come into contact. Hence the ease with which the Russian nature is misunderstood, or only inadequately comprehended by foreigners. Hence, also, the inevitable failure of all attempts to explore the Russian mind or the Russian country, with only French or German for one's interpreter.

Is it not the Russians rather than the English who take their pleasures sadly? Even in the village festivals, the liveliest of all Russian popular out-door enjoyments, there is a lack of earnest merry-making, a want of boisterous joyfulness and *abandon,* almost a shrinking from relaxation and amusement, that leave a painful impression in the mind of the sensitive spectator. . . . On public holidays, or so-called days of national rejoicing, the crowds which closed factories and places of business dismiss to the streets and wear a gloomy and spiritless aspect utterly out of harmony with the idea of out-door enjoyment. On the other hand, enjoyments by *ukaz*, in celebration of events imperial rather than popular in their interest, call forth a most ludicrous half-heartedness on the part of those who participate in them.

A full harvest of pessimism may be gathered by the quiet eye of the stroller through the public gardens of any of the large Russian cities. One of the finest of these resorts is the Lyaytny Sad, or Summer Garden, in St. Petersburg,—a spot of green that in warm weather daily attracts thousands of visitors, and remains full of music and pedestrians long after midnight. Here the crowd is strangely subdued in its manner. Everybody seems absorbed in his own reflections. Army officer, student, *chinovnik*, governess, all wear the same aspect of serious gravity. Couples pass along without seeming to converse; before the orchestra hundreds sit listening, or promenade through the *allée* amid a silence unrelieved by a solitary laugh. Dress deepens the prevailing gloom, since it is characterized by a striking lack of color, most of the women being attired in black. A cemetery might furnish a more convincing proof of the vanity of life, yet it could scarcely attract a crowd more mournful than that which goes its sad, melancholy rounds on summer nights in the Lyaytny Sad.

There is also a noticeable pessimism in nearly all Russian music of a popular or national character. A strange plaintiveness, increased by a frequent resort to the minor key, is heard in countless songs of the people; the effect is often so peculiar that it is difficult to express it even in notes. The saddest of these melodies are sung by students at their gatherings at the university towns; the weirdest, perhaps, take the form of recitative and chorus, heard mostly among the peasants and common people of the country districts. And if Russian music is sad, Russian street cries are infinitely sadder. Anything so mournful as these I never heard. Hour after hour, day after day, with the window of my apartment in the Troitsky Perenlok open upon the quadrangle below, have I listened to the voice of the vender. Sometimes it was a youth, but oftener a man or an old woman, and always the impression has been the same. It was a cry, and yet it seemed a song. And such a song! Heart-piercing it was, and sank into one's soul. It was a shriek of pain, an exclamation of anguish, a wail of despair. It had a life independent of the singer. The vender might go with his basket of wares and return no more, but the lamentation was always rising, and remained ever the same. No single human being, however miserable, I used to think, could have composed it; nor was it the product of any guild, or locality, or even epoch. To me it seemed the rythmic utterance of centuries of suffering. I saw in it, I heard in it, only the accumulated burden of the people's woe condensed into a single cry committed to the keeping of the wretched and the miserable for all time.

27 IMPRACTICABLE VISIONARIES
George Kennan (1845–1924)

A man with very little formal schooling, George Kennan became recognized as the first serious Russian scholar in the United States. Having worked as a telegraph operator since he was twelve, he joined at nineteen an Anglo-American team for surveying a telegraph route across Alaska and Siberia. On the basis of three years' experience in Siberia, he became a well-known lecturer on that region and wrote his widely read book, *Tent Life in Siberia*. Some years later he returned to Russia to travel through the Caucasus. In 1885 he set out again, this time as a journalist, to investigate the prison system in Siberia and the life of the Siberian exiles, who were said to be living under conditions of extreme hardship. A conservative by nature, Kennan was at the beginning of this trip partial to the attempts of the czarist government to maintain order against the revolutionary agitators. His observations, however, led Kennan to different conclusions. His famous reports, which appeared in the *Century Magazine*, roused world opinion against the cruelties of the Russian police state.

Kennan's concern with Russia went beyond such polemical subject matter and encompassed Russian affairs in general. Russia became the object of his abiding interest and study. When asked in which school he had acquired his education, his answer was: "Russia."[105]

His remarks on the Russian character that follow are from an article of 1887 about a visit to Tolstoy.[106]

THE RUSSIAN, as a rule, has a childish faith in the practicability and the speedy realization of plans, hopes, and schemes which an American under precisely similar circumstances, would regard as visionary and quixotic, and would therefore throw aside as having no bearing on his present conduct. When this national trait is united, as it is in the Russian character, with a boundless capacity for self-sacrifice, it brings about results which, to the American mind, are simply bewildering and astonishing. This characteristic which I have called "childishness" is no less apparent in the reasoning and the activity of the Nihilists than in the doctrines and eccentric practices of Count Tolstoi. It was as childish for the Nihilists to suppose that they could attain their objects by assassinating the Tsar as it was for Count Tolstoi to suppose that he could save them from punishment for the act by urging such considerations as the barbarity and sinfulness of the death penalty upon a government which had already shot or hanged fifteen or twenty men for political offenses of less gravity. Both the Nihilists and Count Tolstoi answered affirmatively the question, "Is the proposed method practicable?" The Russian seems to throw himself with a sort of noble, generous, but childish enthusiasm into the most thorny path of self-denial and self-sacrifice, if he can only see, or think that he sees, the shining walls of his ideal golden city at the end of it. He takes no account of difficulties, heeds not the suggestions of prudence, cares not for the natural laws which limit his power, but presses on with a sublime confidence that he can reach the ideal city because he can see it so plainly, and because it is such a desirable city to reach. From Count Tolstoi, striving to bring about the millenium by working for others and sacrificing himself, down to the poor pilgrims by the roadside, striving to better their characters and atone for their sins by laborious pilgrimages to holy shrines, there is manifested this same national characteristic— the disposition to seek desirable ends by inadequate and impracticable methods.

28 BASICALLY AN APOLITICAL PEOPLE

John William Burgess (1844–1931)

A Tennessean, John William Burgess served in the Union army. He studied at Amherst and was later admitted to the Massachusetts bar. He continued his education in Germany, where he did research for George Bancroft and became absorbed in historical studies. He taught history and political science at Amherst, and later he became the first dean of the school of political science at Columbia University. Because of his efforts to establish political science as an independent discipline, he was recognized as the founder of political science in the United States.

His work and friendship with Bancroft and his studies in Germany determined to a great extent his thoughts on the organization of a university, his guide being the German model. His concepts of history and political theory also owed much to his work in Germany and to Bancroft. These included the belief that the "Teutonic race," within which he counted the American people, is superior to others in political capacity. His following views on Russia were published 1890 in a book dealing with problems of political science.[107]

———●———————————————————————●———

To MY MIND the political institution in which the political life of the Greeks incorporated and still incorporates itself is the community. In this the Greek and the Slav agree, and for this reason I treat of them under the same heading. In the organization of the community, the narrowest circle of political life, the political genius of the Greek and Slavonic natures has been chiefly occupied and almost exhausted.

172

According to their political psychology the whole power of the state must be in their community; i.e. the souvereignty must be in the community. Any wider organization could be regarded only as an interstate league, exercising delegated and very limited powers, while the rights of the individuals as against the community could have no existence. In this form of political organization the way lies open for a development, in richest variety, of other qualities of genius, such as music, poetry, art, eloquence, philosophy and religion, provided the germs of the same exist in the psychologic character of the nations; but the race that clings to this form of organization manifests a low order of political genius. Its failings must quickly reveal themselves in political history in three general directions, *viz*; in the poverty and insecurity of individual rights, in the inability to regulate the relations between different communities, and in weakening against external attack. All three of these failings point in the same direction. They make it absolutely necessary that the political organization, in highest instance, of the Greek and Slav nations should be undertaken by a foreign political power. It is no play of chance nor contradiction in character . . . that the Slavs are subject to the autocratic government of the Osmanli and Teutonic dynasties of Rumanoff and Hapsburg. This is the natural result of their want of any comprehensive political genius, and of the exhaustion of their political powers of production in the creation of the lowest forms of political organization. Whether they will ever become educated up to higher degrees of political capacity or are destined permanently to work upon the development of other lines of culture than the political, is, I think, still a question. I do not believe that a consciousness of the political principles which we call modern has been awakened in any considerable number of the Greeks or Slavs, and I do not think that these few more enlightened minds are aware how totally unpolitical their national genius is. They are constantly being disappointed by the want of support from the masses in projects of general reform. I remember some eight years ago a distinguished professor of the University of Moscow, one of the best lawyers and publicists of the Slavic race in Russia, said to me that he expected the Russian revolution to be an accomplished fact before his return to Moscow, which was to be in about six months from the date of this conversation. Time has shown that he was woefully mistaken, and his mistake was in the assumption that the imperial government appeared as unnatural and tyrannic to the mass of Russian subjects as to himself. I do not suppose there is an American schoolboy fifteen years of age, who has not wept bitter tears over the fate of Poland, and who does not think he could reform the government of Russia; and I have no doubt he would begin by dethroning the Czar, abolishing the army and disestablishing the Church; and I am sure that the practical result of the procedure would be that in less than twenty-five years there would be little left of the civilization of Russia and possibly of the civilization of Europe. Let the Caesarism of Russia be made as honest and benevolent as possible, but Caesarism must be the general system of its political organization so long as the political psychology of the Slav is what it is and what it has been.

29 THE HOPE OF A WORLD GROWING EFFETE?

Theodore Roosevelt (1858–1919)

Theodore Roosevelt, the twentieth president of the United States, was much concerned with Russia's position in world politics even before he assumed his high office in 1901. The leader and spokesman of the turn-of-the-century expansionists, he looked at Russia westward, over the Pacific. Events were happening in China: those were the years of the Boxer Rebellion, the opening up of the empire by the European powers, and their struggle for supremacy and predominance in the China trade. The United States' interests favored the open-door policy, in order to prevent control of China by any one of the contending powers, least of all by Russia.

Roosevelt wrote the following letter in 1897,[108] when he was assistant secretary of the navy, to his close friend the British diplomat Cecil Arthur Spring Rice. In it he expressed his view of Russia as a land power that could not "touch" naval powers such as the United States and England. Although he judged the Russians to lag centuries behind the English-speaking nations, he foresaw a great future for them. He considered them, though backward, not as alien barbarians but as Europeans, with perhaps enough of an admixture of barbarian blood to continue the rule of European civilization if and when more effete nations, including the Americans, should fail. While taking into account the possibility that Russia might go her own way, he expected that ultimately, perhaps after a bloody revolution, she would return to the European, liberal fold.

Now, ABOUT THE RUSSIANS, who offer a very much more serious problem than the Germans, if not to our generation, at least to the generation which will succeed us. Russia and the United States are friendly, but Russians and Americans, in their individual capacity, have nothing whatever in common. That they despise Americans in a way is doubtless true. I rather doubt if they despise Europeans. Socially, the upper classes feel themselves akin to other European upper classes, while they have no one to feel akin to in America. Our political corruption certainly cannot shock them, but our political institutions they doubtless both despise and fear. As for our attitude toward them, I don't quite take your view, which seems to be, after all merely a reflection of theirs. Evidently you look upon them as they think they should be looked upon—that is as huge, powerful barbarians, cynically confident that they will in the end inherit the fruits of our civilization, firmly believing that the future belongs to them, and resolute to develop their own form of government, literature and art; despising as effete all of Europe and especially America. I look upon them as a people to whom we can give points, and a beating; a people with a great future, as we have; but a people with poisons working in it, as other poisons, of similar character on the whole, work in us.

Well, there is a certain justification for your view, but the people who have least to fear from the Russians are the people who speak English. They may overrun the continent of Europe, but they cannot touch your people or mine, unless perhaps in India. There is no such difference between them and us as there was between Goths and Byzantines; it will be many a long year before we lose our capacity to lay out those Goths. They are below the Germans just as the Germans are below us; the space between the German and the Russian may be greater than that between the Englishman and the German, but that is all. We are all treading the same path, some faster, some slower; and though the Russian started far behind, yet he has traveled that path very much farther and faster since the days of Elizabeth. He is several centuries behind us still, but he was a thousand years behind us then. He may develop his own art and his own literature, but most assuredly they will be developed on European models and along European lines, and they will differ from those of other European nations no more than Macaulay and Turner differ from Ariosto and Botticelli—nor will his government escape the same fate. While he can keep absolutism, no matter how corrupt, he will himself possess infinite possibilities of menace to his neighbors; but as sure as fate, in the end, when Russia becomes more thickly populated, when Siberia fills with cities and settled districts, the problems which in different forms exist in the free republic of the United States, the free monarchy of England, the free commonwealth of Australia, the unfree monarchy of Prussia, the unfree Republic of France and the heterogeneous empire of Austria, will also have to be faced by the Russian. The nihilist is the socialist or communist in an aggravated form. He makes but a small class; he may temporarily disappear; but his principles will slowly spread. If Russia chooses to develop purely on her own line and to resist the growth of liberalism, she may put off the day of reckoning; but she cannot ultimately avert it, and instead of occasionally having to go through what Kansas has gone through with the populists she will sometime experience a red terror which will make the French Revolution pale. Meanwhile one curious fact is forgotten: The English-speaking people have never gone back before the Slav, and the Slav has never gone back before them save once. Three-quarters of a century ago the Russians meant that Northwestern America should be Russian, and our Monroe Doctrine was formulated as much against them as against the other reactionaries of continental Europe. Now the American has dispossessed the Russian. Thirty years ago there were thirty thousand people speaking more or less Russian in Alaska. Now there are but a few hundreds. The American —the man of the effete English-speaking races—has driven the Slav from the eastern coast of the North Pacific.

What the Russian thinks of us—or indeed what any European thinks of us—is of small consequence. What we *are* is of great consequence; and I wish I could answer you with confidence. Sometimes I do feel inclined to believe that the Russian is the one man with enough barbarous blood in him to be the hope of a world that is growing effete. But I think that this thought comes only when I am unreasonably dispirited.

30 RUSSIA'S DANGER IS FROM THE TOP— THE BOTTOM IS SODDEN

Julian Ralph (1853–1903)

Julian Ralph of New York City was another nineteenth-century newspaperman with a background that may be called "typical." Apprenticed to a printer at the age of fifteen, he worked on newspapers and finally found a job as a reporter for the *Daily Graphic*. His reports of 1875 on the trial of Henry Ward Beecher, who had been accused of adultery, came to the attention of Charles A. Dana. Dana hired Ralph as a reporter for the *Sun*, a job he kept for the next twenty years. Between 1894 and 1897 he traveled through Russia and the Far East. In 1896–1897 he also covered the Turko-Greek War, reporting from the Turkish side of the front lines. Later he worked in London as a correspondent for the *New York Herald* and also for the *Brooklyn Eagle*.

Ralph was said to have had "an uncanny sixth sense that made him anticipate unexpected news." His observations on the passivity of the Russian masses, made in an article of 1898 and presented as the next selection,[109] do not give evidence of that particular faculty. The supposedly "sodden bottom" of Russian society was to show surprising activity during the revolutionary upheavals of 1904–1905, half a dozen years after Ralph saw it as politically inert.

•————————————————————————•

RUSSIA IS A HUGE FARM, comprising a seventh of the land surface of the globe, and a twenty-sixth of its total area. It has half a dozen men to manage it—according to the policy of one of the six—and the people are divided into ten millions of men and women of the more or less comfortable, more or less educated class, and one hundred and nineteen millions of citizens the mass of whom form the dullest, the rudest, least ambitious peasantry in Europe. If one travels over Russia to spy out the land, he may go for days across it from west to east without breaking the continuous view of a flat disk, whose only variety lies between its farmed flatness and its waste flatness, its squat, shrinking, unkempt villages and its sandy districts wooded with their birch and evergreens.

Everywhere it is new, rude, and untidy. . . .

As long as I tried to compare Russia with the countries of the West, and to consider it from a European stand-point, I found myself more than disappointed, almost hostile to it. The sight of the desperately poor millions—unconsidered, non-considering, at rest in their cattle-like condition; the comprehension of the vastness of the gulf between the millions upon millions of them and their few, so-called betters; the shabbiness and want of pride of the soldiers, and the filthiness and dirty quarters of the sailors—these were not comparable with American or European institutions, except at such a disadvantage to Russia as to arouse indignation at the thought that such conditions were the natural outcome of the system of government. . . .

But let the visitor to Russia pursue his comparisons until, as nearly every one fails, he concludes that he must be doing Russia an injustice—until he comes to reflect that the basis and root of its civilization are Asiatic; and not European. Then the task of studying the huge, growing, progressive empire becomes easy and more pleasant at once. Let him once say "Russia is Asiatic," and with the change of his viewpoint he sees everything differently. Then he stops criticising, and begins admiring. He is not in the last and most primitive corner of Europe. He is in the first and most advancing country of Asia.

If any Russian objects to that viewpoint, he will not find fault or contradict if it is said that at least Russia is a land between Europe and Asia.

I considered it Asiatic when its resemblances to what I had seen in other countries of the East forced home the comparison. And from that moment I was able to judge it calmly. In Asia the systems of government are less military, but Russia is forced into militarism by her contact with Europe. The lack of machine-like discipline in the Russian soldiery is truly Asiatic, and so are the stagnation, patience, suffering, and squalor of the people. In Russia they are drunken, instead of being gamblers and opium-smokers as in China. The absence of a middle class and the gulf that takes its place are Asiatic conditions. In Russia no man except a member of the cabinet or a diplomat dares to discuss politics. In other Asiatic countries the people are not forbidden to discuss them, because they have never shown any inclination to do so. No more do the 119,000,000 muzhiks of Russia. Their intellectual activity never goes beyond the affairs of village, family, farm, or employment. Their most active interest is in religion, but they make of that such a mere tissue of forms and mechanical or automatic practices that it is carried on without any more mental effort than the activity of a victim of St. Vitus's dance. The leaven of progress is not in the muzhik any more than it is in the coolie. If Russia's system of government is to be threatened or altered, it must be by the ten million who reflect the European ideals in their dress and manners, and who present fertile ground for the propagation of European reforms—the seeds of which, in the form of free speech and free press and free literature, are denied to them. Russia's danger is from the top; the bottom is sodden.

RUSSIAN STREET SCENE IN WINTER

IMPORTUNING A VISITOR

EFFECTS OF VODKI

PUNISHMENT FOR DRUNKENNESS—SWEEPING THE STREETS

31 THE DANGER LIES IN THE RACE, NOT IN THE CHARACTER OF THE PEOPLE

Frederick Wells Williams (1857–1928)

Williams, a prominent Orientalist, was born in China, the son of an American foreign-service officer and sinologist. After graduating from Yale in 1879, he studied for several years in Germany and France. His early connection with China and the collaboration with his father on what was considered the standard work on China, *Middle Kingdom*, determined his life-long interest in Chinese affairs. During his many years as teacher of Oriental history at Yale, he greatly stimulated and promoted American scholarly occupation with the Far East.

Around the turn of the century Williams was one of a number of influential Americans of patrician background who approved of the growing imperialist involvement of the United States in the Western Hemisphere as well as in the Orient. In an article published in 1899, from which we have selected some excerpts,[110] he proceeded from the assumption that the world was to be ruled by the superior peoples of the white race, the Anglo-Saxons. The Slavs, their contenders, he considered racially and culturally inferior. While he granted the Russians, because of their Aryan descent, certain good qualities, he saw them influenced by the proximity of and adaptation to the inferior Asiatics. The conquest by Russia of the vast population of China could, therefore, pit the retrogressive Asiatic culture against the lofty ideals of the white race, led, as it were, by the Anglo-Saxons.

WHEN WE SEEK for the nation under whose aegis the rote and rule of old Rome may be resuscitated in the near future, only two appear as possible competitors for the grand prize, the Slav and the Anglo-Saxon. These are the only races whose territories and consequently whose potential strength in populations and material resources, are adequate to the stupendous task, whose subjects are colonizers in the true sense that comprises both the peopling of vast spaces and the assimilation and subjection of foreigners to their institutions. These great rivals have been already long at work, each in characteristic fashion, fulfilling what we call, somewhat lightly perhaps, their manifest destiny, each a participator in the conquest of Asia. The solution of the problems seems to lie in their hands, and behind one or the other must sooner or later be ranged all the potential forces of the world.

Superficially both of these colossal empires appear to denote the spirit of the West and all that this implies in the eternal opposition of Orient and Occident, to which allusion has been made. But the accidents of a capital located in Europe and an ancestry traced to a common Aryan origin must not mislead our conclusions. In temperament and propensity these two nations embody the same antagonism that has in times past ranged the civilized world in two hostile camps. Their pretensions are as diverse as those of Persia and Hellendom twenty-two centuries ago—when, too, Aryan chiefs focused and guided the ambitions of East as well as West to different ends. Russia, though arrayed in the panoply of Christendom and bearing the outward symbols of Western culture, is the embodiment and expression of Oriental absolutism, the synonym of obedience to a single will. Great Britain, the present leader of the Anglo-Saxon hosts, is the protagonist of Western conceptions of liberty and self-government. She stands for the freedom of subject as well as souvereign, which, being interpreted in terms made clear by generations of conflict between her own children, means the souvereignty of the subject, of the people. The principles upon which her constitution reposes are the results of centuries of education and evolution in which the races of the East have taken no part.

The past careers of these two aspirants for world-direction furnish a clue to what may logically be expected from them in the future. In the dawn of Slavonic history we find the ancestors of the Russians to be a wayward group of tribes unable to coalesce in effective federation until conquered and given the initiative by an alien power. What the Tartar Bulgars did for some of these clans in the lower Danube valley the Northmen of Scandinavia and the Mongols effected at different times upon other members of the race in Russia. The unity which the Slavs would never of themselves attain was forced upon them from without; but they had their revenge in the end by absorbing their conquerors and reducing their organization to its simplest elements. From this the inference may not unreasonably be made that the Slavic type, though enduring, displays little administrative ability and yields inevitably to the higher political genius of others. It carries its arms far to-day, but its soldiers and colonists bear no new message to the Asiatics with whom they commingle. They overrun their waste places and change their manners and perhaps their language, but for government only offer a Western autocrat in place of an Oriental monarch. It is Asiatic absolutism again incarnate in an Aryan family, as in the days of the Medo-Persian dominion.

The Anglo-Saxon presents a striking contrast in every phase of this comparison. He compels submission not through mere numerical superiority or the primitive process of *force majeur*, but by reason of the inventive and organizing talents of the race. Never content with the experience and example of others, he has worked out his problems to his own satisfaction and impressed his conclusions as a logical necessity upon all with whom he associates. In the light of his past performances it is impossible to imagine that he can ever abandon his ideals or revert to the primitive principles of patriarchal rule. The inevitable outcome of the predominance of one of these two races in Asia is submission to the old-world dogma of divinely-inspired souvereignty, of the other an attempt—it may be altogether in vain—to teach the subject the high doctrine of self-rule. . . .

Russia's objective . . . is international monopoly. Her tendency is toward increased centralization of authority and the concentration of aggressive power whose appetite for territorial extension becomes in the end a mania. There is no place in her scheme for countries that her garrisons do not occupy. To subvert in unending succession, to tax and oppress her subjects for the maintenance of the huge military machine—these are her aims, precisely as they were those of Darius long ago. They involve the suppression of the individual everywhere for the benefit of the ruler, the abasement of the subject, and the inevitable reduction of civilization to a level with the condition of purely military despotisms of the past. She cannot cease aggressions against her neighbors because she is powerless to change her ways and compete with those mercantile nations whose effective conquests are those of peace and the increase of plenty. She frankly and even cynically acknowledges her intention of pushing her acquisitions to the extreme limits of the continent upon which she has entered. She must do so: both to exercise those armies that may, if thwarted, turn and rend her, and to exclude forcibly from those vast spaces the agents of her insatiable commercial adversaries. . . .

The rift in the armor of Russia is the necessity, common to every despotism, of implicit reliance upon those to whom delicate and dangerous tasks are entrusted. Agents who are trained to the sort of business required by irresponsible monarchs will accept the death penalty for failure, they will not tolerate close scrutiny of their accounts. For this reason a habit of corruption has been fostered which the most strenuous absolutism in the world is powerless to keep in check. The vices of bribery and peculation are so generally recognized as prevailing everywhere in the Eastern world that we have come to attribute them, rather loosely and almost unconsciously, to climatic or geographical influences; yet the example of New Japan shows that they are not concomitants to life in the Orient, but are only inevitable to the Oriental system of rule. How deeply this disease of immorality has permeated their society may be inferred from the significant though horrible Russian adage that "Lord Christ himself would steal if his hands were not nailed fast to the cross." . . .

Above all, it is essential to her purpose to secure that richest and most populous realm on earth which has hitherto escaped the hand of the despoiler. Russia's need of China does not at all imply a necessity for increased markets to satisfy the desires of an overflowing industrial population. It means the direct increase of her fighting force by the acquisition of millions of hardy peasants who can, under European training, be turned into admirable soldiers; it represents the addition to her already magnificent resources of the richest mineral deposits to be found anywhere in the world; it signifies to her manufacturing rival that these supplies of men and material are to be henceforth as in the past withdrawn from the general service of mankind and reserved for her exclusive benefit. With the immoderate power involved in the mastery of these possessions, extending over a wide and continuous domain, impenetrable from without, but made articulate within by methods which modern science provides, Russia will have only to issue commands while the inhabitants of the earth tremble and obey. For it must not be forgotten that her peculiar strength depends upon positions as well as upon size. With her back to the frozen ocean and her feet planted firmly upon two continents, she occupies a strategic front that can be maintained against any assault. Add to this the natural wealth from the mines and fields and manual labor of Asia, and the result is a combination of potency and energy that not only defies attack, but eventually threatens destruction to every other existing political power. Upon the highlands of Central Asia have been bred in the past the races which overran and dominated the civilized West, and where these swarms were once raised other millions may spring up in the future to obey the call of the conqueror and spread devastation among those more cultured but less lusty people who represent our race. It might indeed be an interesting speculation to calculate the chances of Africa, Australia and the two Americas if pitted against a united Russian-Asia, in some supreme encounter a century or two hence. . . .

Russia with the confidence of a youthful and courageous savage intends to pursue her passion for omnipotence to the very end. A less rudimentary racial type would long since have been diverted from this artless ambition by the complex distractions of an inventing and speculative age; an older people would not have dared. In her indifference to the risk incurred, in the crudity of her ideals, in her deliberate preference for the ruthless way of the ancient East, lie the menace of her pretensions. The conclusion to the conquest already begun between Asia and Europe under Slav or Saxon leadership allows no alternative between victory on the one side and destruction on the other. . . .

It is imperative to comprehend fully the purport of this great question and discern the abyss that yawns beyond. Nor is it necessary to defame the Russian character in order to strengthen the protest against these assumptions. It is in the race tendency rather than in the people themselves that the danger lies. They have often and beneficially played the rôle of civilizers in the darkest Asia, enforcing peace and good order where none had been known for centuries. Their work in reducing the khanates of Turkestan and compelling the desert slavers there to forego their favorite activities of kidnapping and robbery, compares favorably with anything that England has done of the same sort. In dealing with the ruder Asiatic they undoubtedly succeeded better than their less pliant rivals, the English; and by reason of the personal popularity of their administrators, as well as because of the prestige of their unbroken successes, they enjoy a fairer prospect of securing the guidance of militant Asia by choice of the fighting class than any other foreign folk. Yet it is this very *simpatica* [sic] with a grosser civilization that befits their Aryan descent that constitutes the gravity of the impending crisis. It shows that half-measures and a merely superficial modification of barbaric society satisfy the Russian conscience. It proves again, if additional proof be needed, that the Slav is ready in all that touches and inspires the soul of a nation to sink to the low level of Asiatic ideals, to surrender what he has learned from liberal Europe and relapse into the animalism and inertness of Oriental life. And when the mark of his European culture, brandished a little contemptuously now before our eyes, is at length thrown aside, we shall find ourselves, while opposed to this Caliban of to-day confronted with the old, unchanging issue of Eastern tyranny and retrogression *versus* Western freedom and progress.

To keep this prototype of brute force from pervading and controlling the whole world, the nations that still cherish lofty hopes for humanity must forget their sectionalism and stand together in battle.

32 GLOSSY POLISH HIDES SAVAGE VIGOR

Carl Schurz (1829–1906)

Born and educated in Germany, Carl Schurz had been involved in the revolutionary activities of 1848 and was forced to flee his native country. In 1851 he arrived in the United States and ultimately settled in Madison, Wisconsin. As a member of the Republican party, he continued his political interests in his adopted country. He opened a law practice in Milwaukee, but in 1860 Abraham Lincoln sent him to Spain as the American minister. He resigned that post in order to become an officer in the Civil War. After the war he returned to politics. He was active as a newspaper editor and a highly reputed public speaker. Aside from writing numerous articles, particularly for *Harper's*, he published biographies of Henry Clay and of Abraham Lincoln.

His prophetic remarks on Russia and the Russian Revolution were written in 1900.[111] They are based on conversations he had in 1855 with Russian émigrés in London.

———————●———————

IT WAS on the occasion of this sojourn in London that I made the acquaintance of Alexander Herzen, a natural son of a Russian nobleman of high rank, himself a Russian patriot in the liberal sense, who had been obliged to leave his native country as a "dangerous man," and who now, by his writings, which were smuggled across the frontier, worked to enlighten and stimulate and inspire the Russian mind. Malwida von Meysenbug, who lived in his family superintending the education of his daughters, which she did with all her

190

peculiar enthusiasm, brought us together, and we soon became friends. Herzen, at least ten years older than I, was an aristocrat by birth and instinct, but a democrat by philosophy, a fine, noble nature, a man of culture, of a warm heart and large sympathies. In his writings as well as in his conversation he poured forth his thoughts and feelings with an impulsive, sometimes poetic eloquence, which, at times, was exceedingly fascinating. I would listen to him by the hour when in his rhapsodic way he talked of Russia and the Russian people, that uncouth and only half conscious giant, that would gradually exchange its surface civilization borrowed from the West for one of national character; the awakening of whose popular intelligence would then put an end to the stolid autocracy, the deadening weight of which held down every free aspiration; and which then would evolve from its mysterious depths new ideas and forces which might solve many of the problems now perplexing the Western world. But, in his fervid professions of faith in the greatness of that destiny, I thought I discovered an undertone of doubt, if not despondency, as to the possibilities of the near future, and I was strongly reminded of the impression made upon me by some of Turguéneff's novels describing Russian society as it entertained itself with vague musings and strivings of dreary aimlessness.

Other impressions I gathered through my contact with some of Herzen's Russian friends who from time to time met in his hospitable house and at his table. At dinner the conversation would sparkle with dramatic tales of Russian life, descriptions of weird social conditions and commotions, which opened mysterious prospects of great upheavings and transformations, and which were interspersed with witty sallies against the government and droll satires on the ruling classes. But when, after dinner, the bowl of strong punch was put on the table, the same persons, who, so far, at least had conducted themselves like gentlemen of culture and refinement, becoming gradually heated, would presently break out in ebullitions of a sort of savage wildness, the like of which I had never witnessed among Germans, or French, or English, or Americans. They strongly reminded me of the proverb: "You scratch a Russian, and you find a Tartar."

Herzen himself always remained self-contained; but as an indulgent host he did not restrain his guests. Probably he knew that he could not. Once or twice he would say to me in an undertone, witnessing my amazement: "So they are! So they are! But they are splendid fellows for all that." And so, I suppose, they are indeed, not only as individuals but as a nation—a huge, unshapely mass, with a glossy polish on the outer surface, but fierce forces within, kept in control by a tremendous pressure of power, or superstition, or stolid faith, but really untamed and full of savage vigor. If they once break loose, awful cataclysms must result, producing in their turn—what? It is difficult to imagine how the Russian empire as it now is, from Poland to eastern-most Siberia, could be kept together and governed by anything else than autocratic centralization of power, a constantly self-asserting and directing central authority with a tremendous organization of force behind it. The rigid central despotism cannot fail to create oppressive abuses in the government of the various territories and diverse populations composing the empire. When this burden of oppression becomes too galling, efforts, raw, crude, more or less inarticulate and confused, will be made in quest of relief, with a slim chance of success. Discontent with the inexorable autocracy will spread and will seize upon the superior intelligence of the country, which will be inspired with the restless ambition to have a share in the government.

At the moment when the autocrat yields to the demands of that popular intelligence and assents to constitutional limitations of his power, or to anything that will give an authoritative, official voice to the people, the real revolutionary crisis will begin. The popular discontent will not be appeased, but it will be sharpened by the concession. All the social forces will then be thrown into spasmodic commotion; and, when those forces, in their native wildness, break through their traditional restraints, the world may have to witness a spectacle of revolutionary chaos without example in history. The chaos may ultimately bring forth new conceptions of freedom, right, and justice, new forms of organized society, new developments of civilization. But what the sweep of those volcanic disturbances will be and what their final outcome, is a mystery baffling the imagination—a mystery that can be approached only with awe and dread.*

Such were the contemplations set going in my mind by the contact with this part of the Russian world, that enigma of the future. With what delightful assurance I returned from this cloudy puzzle to the "New World" which I had recently made my home—the great western Republic, not indeed without its hard problems, but a Republic founded upon clear, sound, just, humane, irrefragable principles, the conscious embodiment of the highest aims of the modern age.

* The above was written in 1900, four years before the revolutionary out-break in Russia.—C. S.

33 NOTHING IN COMMON WITH ANY ANCIENT OR MODERN WORLD

Henry Adams (1838–1918)

Henry Adams, coming from one of the first families of the United States, was a great-grandson of John Adams, the second president, and grandson of John Quincy Adams, the sixth president. Henry had served as secretary to his father, Charles Francis, American ambassador to England. But the prominent participation in the political life of the nation, a family tradition, ended with his generation. Henry, as well as his brothers Charles Francis and Brooks, became a historian, a career he considered as a failure because of the high expectations of leadership that he thought his famous name implied. Posterity did not agree with his judgment. The value of his books, *The Life of Gallatin* and *History of the United States during the Administrations of Jefferson and Madison*, continue to be recognized. His observations on Russia are from his autobiography, *The Education of Henry Adams*, which, since it was first issued in 1907, has become an American classic.[112]

In 1901 Henry traveled to Russia in the company of Henry Cabot Lodge, the senator from Massachusetts. Two years earlier he had written to his brother Brooks that he did not want to go to Russia for at least ten years, at which time he would be able to observe the impact of Western technology on the backward country. Moreover, he wrote, "I loathe the country and the people."[113] But when he got to see the Russians at close range, he found them "fascinating" and "wonderful," even though he did not evaluate them as individuals. For Henry Adams, the Russian peasant was the representative of the race, of an archaic society. In accordance with his mechanistic theory of history, he saw in the Russian peasantry a passive mass whose inert weight and negative energy, once it was propelled forward by the technical advances of the twentieth century, would engulf Europe and become a threat also to the United States. In the meantime, "for a hundred years, at least, Russia and we ought to be friends without trying. We have next to nothing in common except our size."[114]

———————————————————————

IN AMERICA all were conservative Christian anarchists; the faith was national, racial, geographic. The true American had never seen such supreme virtue in any of the innumerable shades between social anarchy and social order as to mark it exclusively human and its own. He never had known a complete union either in Church or State or thought, and had never seen any need for it. The freedom gave him courage to meet any contradiction, and intelligence enough to ignore it. Exactly the opposite condition had marked Russian growth. The Czar's empire was a phase of conservative Christian anarchy more interesting to history than all the complex variety of American newspapers, schools, trusts, sects, frauds, and Congressmen. These were Nature—pure and anarchic as the conservative Christian anarchist saw Nature—active, vibrating, mostly unconscious, and quickly reacting on force; but, from the first glimpse one caught from the sleeping-car window, in the early morning, of the Polish Jew at the accidental railway station, in all his weird horror, to the last vision of the Russian peasant, lighting his candle and kissing his ikon before the railway Virgin in the station at St. Petersburg, all was logical, conservative, Christian and anarchic. Russia had nothing in common with any ancient or modern world that history knew; she had been the oldest source of all civilization in Europe, and had kept none for herself; neither Europe nor Asia had ever known such a phase, which seemed to fall into no line of evolution whatever, and was as wonderful to the student of Gothic architecture in the twelfth century, as to the student of the dynamo in the twentieth. Studied in the dry light of conservative Christian anarchy, Russia became luminous like the salt of radium; but with a negative luminosity as though she were a substance whose energies had been sucked out—an inert residuum—with movement of pure inertia. From the car window one seemed to float past undulations of nomad life—herders deserted by their leaders and herds—wandering waves stopped in their wanderings—waiting for their winds or warriors to return and lead them westward; tribes that had camped, like Khirgis, for the season, and had lost the means of motion without acquiring the habit of permanence. They waited and suffered. As they stood they were out of place, and could never have been normal. Their country acted as a sink of energy like the Caspian Sea, and its surface kept the uniformity of ice and snow. One Russian peasant kissing an ikon on a saint's day, in the Kremlin, served for a hundred million. The student had no need to study Wallace, or re-read Tolstoy or Tourguenieff or Dostoiewski to refresh his memory of the most poignant analysis of human inertia ever put in words; Gorky was more than enough: Kropotkin answered every purpose.

The Russian people could never have changed—could they ever be changed? Could inertia of race, on such a scale, be broken up, or take new form? Even in America, on an infinitely smaller scale, the question was old and unanswered. All the so-called primitive races, and some nearer survivals, had raised doubts which persisted against the most obstinate convictions of evolution. The Senator himself shook his head, and after surveying Warsaw and Moscow to his content, went on to St. Petersburg to ask questions of Mr. de Witte and Prince Khilkoff. Their conversations add new doubts; for their efforts had been immense, their expenditure enormous, and their results on the people seemed to be uncertain as yet, even to themselves. Ten or fifteen years of violent stimulus seemed resulting in nothing, for, since 1898, Russia lagged.

The tourist-student, having duly reflected, asked the Senator whether he should allow three generations, or more, to swing the Russian people into the Western movement. The Senator seemed disposed to ask for more. The student had nothing to say. For him, all opinion founded on fact must be error, because the facts can never be complete, and their relations must be always infinite. Very likely, Russia would instantly become the most brilliant constellation of human progress through all the ordered stages of good; but meanwhile one might give a value as movement of inertia to the mass, and assume a slow acceleration that would, at the end of a generation, leave the gap between east and west relatively the same. . . .

Until the student is fairly sure that his problem is soluble, he gains little by obstinately insisting on solving it. One might doubt whether Mr. de Witte himself, or Prince Khilkoff, or any Grand Duke, or the Emperor, knew much more about it than their neighbors; and Adams was quite sure that, even in America, he should listen with uncertain confidence to the views of any Secretary of the Treasury, or railway president, or President of the United States whom he had ever known, that should concern the America of the next generation. The mere fact that any man should dare to offer them would prove his incompetence to judge. Yet Russia was too vast a force to be treated as an object of unconcern. As inertia, if in no other way, she represented three fourths of the human race, and her movement might be the true movement of the future, against the hasty and unsure acceleration of America. . . .

As [he] looked back across the Baltic from the safe battlements of Stockholm, Russia looked more portentous than from the Kremlin.

The image was that of the retreating ice-cap—a wall of archaic glacier, as fixed, as ancient, as eternal, as the wall of archaic ice that blocked the ocean a few hundred miles to the northward, and more likely to advance. Scandinavia had been ever at its mercy. Europe had never changed. The imaginary line that crossed the level continent from the Baltic to the Black Sea, merely extended the northern barrier-line. The Hungarians and the Poles on one side still struggled against the Russian inertia of race, and retained their own energies under the same conditions that caused inertia across the frontier. Race ruled the conditions; conditions hardly affected race; and yet no one could tell the patient tourist what race was, or how it should be known. History offered a feeble and delusive smile at the sound of the word; evolutionists and ethnologists disputed its very existence; no one knew what to make of it; yet, without the clue, history was a nursery tale.

The Germans, Scandinavians, Poles and Hungarians, energetic as they were, had never held their own against the heterogeneous mass of inertia called Russia, and trembled with terror whenever Russia moved. From Stockholm one looked back on it as though it were an ice-sheet, and so had Stockholm watched it for centuries. In contrast with the dreary forests of Russia and the stern streets of St. Petersburg, Stockholm seemed a southern vision. . . .

. . . To recover his grasp of chaos, he must look back across the gulf to Russia, and the gap seemed to have suddenly become an abyss. Russia was infinitely distant. Yet the nightmare of the glacial ice-cap still pressed down on him from the hills, in full vision, and no one could look out on the dusky and oily sea that lapped these spectral islands without consciousness that only a day's steaming to the northward would bring him to the ice-barrier, ready at any moment to advance, which obliged tourists to stop where Laps and reindeer and Norse fishermen had stopped so long ago that memory of their very origin was lost. Adams had never before met a *ne plus ultra*, and knew not what to make of it; but he felt at least the emotion of his Norwegian fishermen ancestors, doubtless numbering hundreds of thousands, jammed with their faces to the sea, the ice on the north, the ice-cap of Russian inertia pressing from behind, and the ice a trifling danger compared with the inertia. From the day they first followed the retreating ice-cap round the North Cape, down to the present moment, their problem was the same.

34 DECADENT CHILDREN OF BYZANTIUM
Henry Cabot Lodge (1850–1924)

Henry Cabot Lodge, the patrician from Boston, was generally known as the conservative Republican senator from Massachusetts, the isolationist adversary of President Wilson. Prior to entering politics, he had completed law school, edited the *North American Review* for a number of years, and lectured on American history at Harvard. He was a close friend of Theodore Roosevelt, with whom he shared a belief in the superiority of the Anglo-Saxons and a commitment to American expansionism. Such a commitment was quite a contrast to the narrow isolationism of his later years.

In 1901 Lodge traveled to Russia, accompanied by Henry Adams. On the basis of that trip Lodge published in 1902 an essay from which the following excerpts have been selected.[115] As Henry Adams reported, he "asked the Senator whether he should allow three generations, or more, to swing the Russian people into the Western movement. The Senator seemed disposed to ask for more." Lodge believed that the Russians had a great future. For the present, however, Russia seemed to him a country of political "decadence," because the people were devoted to an all-powerful man, not to a government of laws. In contrast to Theodore Roosevelt, he thought of the Russian people and civilization as completely alien and, in fact, Oriental. In tracing the Western political organization to Rome and that of Russia to Byzantium, he overlooked that the Western Roman Empire had declined into a decadent Caesarean rule as had the Eastern. Moreover, Lodge equated Byzantium with "decadence," which was the custom at that time when the cultural achievements of the Byzantine period were largely unknown.

IT IS TRUE that, owing to the superior energy of the American people, a long interval still separates us from Russia. . . . But none the less Russia has the natural resources,—she has, like ourselves, a large future; her natural resources are still undeveloped. The nations which have hitherto held economic supremacy, but whose natural resources have begun to contract and decline, demand, no doubt, our most watchful attention, but need not excite our apprehension. Ultimate peril, if there is any, can only come from a nation of the future, with possibilities as yet unmeasured and unknown.

To every reflecting American, therefore, Russia is of absorbing interest, not only on account of the friendship she has frequently shown us, but because she is potentially an economic rival more formidable than any other organized nation. . . . That which it concerns us to know is how far this great country and its resources are now developed, whether they can be fully and effectively developed by the Russian people, and, if so, how soon they will reach the point of dangerous and destructive rivalry. . . .

To a native of western Europe or of the United States, the first feeling which masters him in Russia is that he has come among a people whose fundamental ideas, whose theory of life, and whose controlling motives of action are utterly alien to his own. There is no common ground, no common starting-place, no common premise of thought and action. The fact that the Russians on the surface and in external things are like us, only accentuates the underlying and essential differences. In all the outward forms of social life, in the higher education, in methods of intercourse both public and private, they do not differ from us, and Peter's imitative policy has in all these things been carried to completion. That the man in the breech-clout, that the wearer of the turban or the pigtail, should be wholly alien to us is so obvious that we are not startled. But that men who in the world of society and in the cities dress like us and have our manners should be at the bottom so utterly different, gives a sharp and emphatic jar to all one's preconceived ideas.

It is always difficult to state in a few words the radical differences which separate one people from another in thought and habits, in the conduct and ideals of life. But here the past helps us to a definition at once broad and suggestive. We are the children of Rome, and the Russians are the children of Byzantium. Between Rome, republican or imperial, and its Greek successor at Byzantium there was a great gulf fixed. One was Latin, the other was the Greek of decadence and subjection. One was Western, the other was Eastern. Ideas inherited from Rome permeated western Europe and were brought thence to America. From Rome comes our conception of patriotism, to take but a single example, that love of country which made Rome what she was in her great days. The patriotism of a Russian applies only to the Tsar. . . . That which moves an American, an Englishman, a Frenchman, or a German to heroic deeds is devotion to his native land, to his fatherland, to that ideal entity which is known as "country." That which moves the Russian is devotion to a man who, next to God, commands his religious faith and stands to him for his country. The first conception is Roman, and of the Western World. The second is Oriental, and pertains to the subtle Greek intellect in its decadence. . . .

The great central idea that the Tsar not only represents God on earth, but that he owns country and people, is still dominant and controlling. In other words, the State, in the person of the Tsar, is owner and master, and the result is a military and religious socialism which is economically a wasteful and clumsy system, utterly unable to compete against the intense individualism of other countries working through highly perfected and economical organizations. The same difference of feeling as to the relations of men may be seen in everything. The religious obeisance of the Russians, for example, with its crouching attitude and the head touching the pavement is thoroughly Oriental, and never was known in any Western Church. One feels at every step the great gulf fixed between those who inherit the ideas of Roman law, liberty, and patriotism, and those who still hold to the slavish doctrines of the Greek Empire of Byzantium.

35 IN RUSSIA A GREAT MAN MAY DO GREAT THINGS

Andrew Dickson White (1832–1918)

During his long, active life, Andrew Dickson White combined a successful academic career with one in diplomacy. Like so many nineteenth-century American intellectuals, he completed his studies in Europe, in his case, at the universities of Berlin and Paris. In an interval in his years of European studies, he served as attaché of the United States legation at St. Petersburg during the Crimean War. After teaching history and English literature, he became active in New York state politics, his primary interests being the reform of municipal administration and of public education. To him can be credited the founding of Cornell University. He became its first president and a professor of history. His many years at Cornell were interrupted by his appointment as minister to Germany (1879–1881) and to Russia at St. Petersburg (1892–1894). Later he returned to Germany as the American ambassador. The founder of the American Historical Association, he served as its first president.

During his years in Russia he enjoyed extensive social contacts among the nobility and in court circles. This influenced his early views on Russia, in which he relied on "the patriarchal democratic system," the "noble breed" of the vast mass of the people, and the "sound mind of the Indo-Germanic races," for the progress of the country.[116] As can be seen in this selection from his autobiography of 1905,[117] he changed his opinion during the events of 1904 and 1905, blaming the lack of free discussion and of an unfettered public opinion for the ills of society and for the extremist positions of many of Russia's great men.

OF ALL DISTINGUISHED MEN that I have ever met, Tolstoi seems to me most in need of that enlargement of view and healthful modification of opinion which come from meeting men and comparing views with them in different lands and under different conditions. This need is all the greater because in Russia there is no opportunity to discuss really important questions. Among the whole one hundred and twenty million people there is no public body in which the discussion of large public questions is allowed; the press affords no real opportunity for discussion; indeed, it is more than doubtful whether such discussion would be allowed to any effective extent even in private correspondence or at one's own fireside. . . .

Like so many other men of genius in Russia, then,—and Russia is fertile in such,—Tolstoi has had little opportunity to take part in any real discussion of leading topics; and the result is that his opinions have been developed without modification by any rational interchange of thought with other men. Under such circumstances any man, no matter how noble or gifted, having given birth to striking ideas, coddles and pets them until they become the full-grown, spoiled children of his brains. He can at last see neither spot or blemish in them, and comes virtually to believe himself infallible. This characteristic I found in several other Russians of marked ability. Each had developed his theories for himself until he had become infatuated with them, and despised everything differing from them.

This is the main cause why sundry ghastly creeds, doctrines, and sects—religious, social, political and philosophic—have been developed in Russia. . . .

In social creeds they have developed nihilism, which virtually assumes the right of an individual to sit in judgment upon the whole human race and condemn to death every other human being who may differ in opinion or position from this self-constituted judge.

In political creed they have conceived the monarch as the all-powerful and irresponsible viceregent of God, and all the world outside of Russia as given over to Satan, for the reason that it has "rejected the divine principle of Authority."

In various branches of philosophy they have developed doctrines which involve the rejection of the best to which man has attained in science, literature, and art, and a return to barbarism.

In the theory of life and duty they have devised a pessimistic process under which the human race would cease to exist.

Every one of these theories is the outcome of some original mind of more or less strength, discouraged, disheartened, and overwhelmed by the sorrows of Russian life; developing its ideas logically and without any possibility of adequate discussion with other men. . . .

During two centuries Russia has been coming slowly out of the middle ages—indeed, out of perhaps the most cruel phases of medieval life. Her history is, in its details, discouraging; her daily life is disheartening. Even the aspects of nature are to the last degree depressing; no mountains; no hills; no horizon; no variety in forests; a soil during a large part of the year frozen or parched; a people whose upper classes are mainly given up to pleasure and whose lower classes are sunken in fetishism; all their poetry and music in the minor key; old oppressions of every sort still lingering; no help in sight; and, to use their own cry, "God so high and the Czar so distant."

When, then, a great man arises in Russia, if he gives himself wholly to some well-defined purpose, looking to one high aim and rigidly excluding sight or thought of the ocean of sorrow about him, he may do great things. If he be Suvaroff or Skobeleff or Gourko he may win great battles; if he be Mendeléieff he may reach some epoch-making discovery in science; if he be Derjavine he may write a poem like the "Ode to God"; if he be Antokolsky he may carve statues like "Ivan the Terrible"; if he be Nesselrode he may hold all Europe enchained to the ideas of an autocrat; if he be Miloutine or Samarine or Tscherkavsky he may devise vast plans like those which enabled Alexander II to free twenty millions of serfs and to secure means of subsistence for each of them; if he be Prince Khilkoff he may push railway systems over Europe to the extremes of Asia; if he be DeWitte he may reform a vast financial system.

But when a strong genius in Russia throws himself into philan-thropic speculations of an abstract nature, with no chance of discussing his theories until they are full-grown and have taken fast hold upon him—if he be a man of science like Prince Kropotkin, one of the most gifted scientific thinkers of our time,—the result may be a wild revolt, not only against the whole system of his own country, but against civilization itself, and finally the adoption of the theory and practice of anarchism, which logically results in the destruction of the entire human race. Or, if he be an accomplished statesman and theologian like Pobodonostyeff, he may reason himself back into medieval methods, and endeavor to fetter all free thought and to crush out all forms of Christianity except the Russo-Greek creed and ritual. Or, if he be a man of the highest genius in literature, like Tolstoi, whose native kindliness holds him back from the extremes of nihilism, he may rear a fabric heaven-high, in which truths, errors, and paradoxes are piled up together until we have a new Tower of Babel.

36 THERE IS A PECULIAR GENTLENESS IN THE RUSSIAN NATURE

Herbert H. D. Peirce (1849–1916)

A descendant of an old New England family with strong ties to Harvard, Peirce entered that school. He left it to embark upon a business career but ended up in the diplomatic service. From 1894 to 1898 he was secretary and chargé d'affaires of the legation at St. Petersburg. As third assistant secretary of state he participated in the Russo-Japanese peace conference at Portsmouth, New Hampshire. After a tour of duty in Norway, he was assigned in 1915 to St. Petersburg, this time as minister plenipotentiary and assistant ambassador.

Peirce is said to have been a courteous man with artistic tastes. He seems to have been concerned also with social issues, as revealed in his sympathetic views of the Russian peasant and his problems. Before 1905 he considered, like so many others, the peasant to be "accustomed to look to the sense of equity in his souvereign and his souvereign's servants . . . confident in the paternal regard" for his rights and welfare.[118] The events of 1904–1905 seem to have led him to modify his views, which becomes apparent in the last part of this excerpt from an article published in 1906.[119]

●————————————————————————————————————●

THERE IS a peculiar gentleness in the Russian nature, whether it is that of the noble or of the peasant, which shows itself in the treatment of animals and of children. True, wife-beating is not uncommon among mujiks, but it is not of an excessively brutal type,

206

and all the songs and traditions of the people show that the woman regards it as part of her necessary lot. Herberstein, the first ambassador from any western state to Russia, narrates an incident which came under his observation. A German, living in Moscow, had married a Russian woman who complained to her liege lord that he did not love her. To his inquiry how he had failed in his affections she replied that he never beat her. Whereupon he commenced the practice and finally killed her.

On the other hand, even when inflamed by intoxication, the mujik rarely becomes pugnacious. His drunkenness takes the form, more ordinarily, of maudlin sentimentality or absolute stupor. While drunkenness is common among the mujik both in town and country, it is not apt to be so often habitual as had been depicted. On occasions of fêtes, of which, unhappily there are many in Russia, the holidays in the year numbering over ninety, it is not uncommon for all the male inhabitants in a country village to get drunk, but the habit of daily drunkenness is not common. . . .

While the mujik is extremely devout and deeply imbued with the spirit of reverence, his highly emotional religious belief is strangely mixed with the pagan legends of a previous time. . . .

The ordinary view of the peasant regarding Divine interference in human affairs, is that, if God only knew his sufferings he would relieve them, but that the priest is indifferent, or by reason of his immorality has no influence with the saints, and so the Almighty is kept in ignorance of his needs, as is the Tsar by the Tchinovicks who surround him. He believes, therefore, that what has been ordained, will happen and that it is useless for him to attempt to change the course of events; hence his lack of forethought for the future.

If some piece of temporary good fortune comes to him, as a gift of money, he accepts it gladly and quickly squanders it, while if misfortune comes, his elastic nature enables him soon to forget and to accept patiently his hard lot in life. It is in this spirit that heretofore he has accepted the obligation imposed upon him by the government to pay for the land which he believes is of right his own. He is convinced that the tax is an unauthorized one, collected by a corrupt bureaucracy for its own profit.

In honesty, the mujik will, on the whole, compare favorably with the peasants of other countries. It is a fact that he inherits certain of the traditions of serfdom when, as the property of the landholder and part of the estate, he believes it is right to take to himself for his own use that which belongs to his master. If, for instance, he were hungry and lacked food, he would not hesitate to take it from his owner. If to-day, in the cultivation of the property of the landholder on the share system, he finds some implement useful, he does not hesitate to appropriate it for the cultivation of that land; but theft of money or valuables in the ordinary sense is rare among the mujik class in town or country. . . .

The mujik is usually depicted as not only illiterate and steeped in the deepest ignorance, but as incapable of intelligent reasoning. This is far from being a fair estimate of either his acquirements or his capabilities. It is true that the peasants in the remote districts and often, indeed, in more accessible parts of the Empire, are wholly illiterate, but in the larger towns, where education is easily obtainable, and in not a few country districts, they often get a very fair common school education. It is by no means rare to find the son of a petty tradesman speaking four languages with considerable fluency. However illiterate and wherever found, he shows considerable acumen in dealing with questions which pertain to the management of matters of which he has a fair understanding. While slow to grasp a new idea, in the ordinary matters of the commune, for instance, he shows no little hardheaded sense. Once convinced of the truth of his point of view it is difficult by arguments to shake his faith. He is emotionally conservative and holds tenaciously to all his beliefs. . . .

The orthodox peasant is as little accustomed to question governmental or religious questions, holding equally to his faith in God and in the Tsar. If he has therefore submitted to what he regards as the oppression of the bureaucracy, it is because he has seen no way of combating it. Once, however, convince him that he has rights which by exertion he can obtain, and he becomes a fanatic pressing on with irresistible force to the attainment of his end, as the recent strikes have demonstrated.

RUSSIAN PEASANT GIRL

RUSSIAN PEASANTS AT THEIR RECREATION

TOLSTOY AND GORKY: THE DECLINE
OF THE NOBILITY AND THE RISE OF
THE LOWER CLASSES
Archibald John Wolfe (1878–1934)

Archibald John Wolfe, born in Vienna, came to the United States as a
young man. After attending courses at the Cincinnati Law School, he
entered the business world, working mainly with export-trade organizations. During several periods he served in the foreign-trade section
of the United States Department of Commerce, which assigned him
from 1911 to 1913 to work in Europe and the Near East. In 1916 he
spent some time in St. Petersburg as a representative of American
steel interests. After rejoining the Department of Commerce from
1921 to 1925, he worked again with organizations promoting foreign
trade. He became widely known in business circles as a lecturer, as
the author of numerous articles about foreign trade, and as the editor
of periodicals in that field.

Along with these pursuits, Wolfe had a deep interest in Russian
literature. In 1916 he interrupted his business activities to devote
himself exclusively to his avocation. The results were translations
of works by Tolstoy and Andreyev. His article of 1908 in *The
Sewanee Review*,[120] which is reprinted here, is his first-known contribution to the field of Russian letters. In it he established, with
unusual perception, an interesting parallel between sociopolitical
developments and literary trends. A decade before the revolution he
understood that Russian literature would evolve from Tolstoy's
moralistic novels into politically inspired writing that would function
as a weapon in the hands of movements trying to shape a new day.

At the same time, however, Wolfe pointed toward "other movements, other influences," which were indeed to find artistic expression in a "new, but still original form" before the progression from moralism and social criticism led eventually to socialist realism.

•────────────────────────────•

IN THE PERSONS of the two foremost living representatives of Russian literature—Count Leo Tolstoy and Maxim Gorky—we see two elements which have influenced its progress: the landed nobility and the proletary. The first, indeed, has already advanced to the extreme limit (at least outwardly) of that tendency which characterizes the latter period of the autocratic domination in Russian literature and which may be expressed in the motto "Back to the soil," while in Gorky, the upstart, the man from nowhere, the proletary looms in the foreground.

If one recalls the Dantesque scenes of "In a Night Lodging-House," ... one is not prepared to realize the fact that the literature of Russia is a nursling of blue-blooded aristocracy. Pushkin had behind him six hundred years of titled ancestry; Plestscheeff was a descendant of the saintly Metropolitan Alexis; Tolstoy's titles date back two hundred years; Lermontoff, Turgeneff, Hertzen, Granoffsky, Saltykoff, Ogareff—all are scions of old nobility; Koltsoff, Belinsky, Polevoy, all are noblemen.

A noted Russian critic remarks that for forty years, from 1820 to 1860, not only every writer, but every hero of Russian fiction was a nobleman, and the peculiar psychology of the Russian nobleman and serf-owner was not only reflected but also fully expressed in Russian literature.

While the Russian nobility as such was stubbornly opposed to progress in any shape or form, the foremost Russian fighters for liberty on the battlefield whereon the pen is the weapon, were men like Tolstoy, brought up in an atmosphere where the peculiar type of the Russian lord and as characteristic a type of the Russian serf combined together in a strange union and affected every expression of public and private activity. "We are slaves," writes Hertzen, "be-

cause our fathers had sold their human dignity for inhuman privileges, and we are enjoying them. We are slaves because we are
masters. We are servants because we're self-owners and serf-owners
without belief in our right to be such. We are serfs because we keep
in a state of serfdom our brothers, our equals by birth, by blood, by
language." The serfs and serf-owners created the literature of Russia.

What was the character of that Russian nobility? Outwardly it
only faintly resembled the feudal system of Western Europe. In the
privacy of its estates it led a life of shameful and vulgar idleness, of
dissolute license, and it exhibited a simply incredible cruelty to serfs.
A sense of duty, a struggle for rights, a knightly romanticism and the
adventures of chivalry—in short, all that went to beautify Western
feudalism remained foreign to Russian nobility. In the seventeenth
century the titled landowner in Russia was either a tamed prince or
a favored ennobled commoner, but in either case devoted to his
supreme lord and busily exploiting his serfs. Russian nobility was not
the child of conquests, but developed on the basis of a systematic
and progressive enslavement of peasantry.

While the history of the West progressed from one madness to
another, and from crusades to humanism, science and discoveries,
Russia knew few madnesses and few intellectual epidemics. Even
the growth of dissent failed to awaken the Russian. The dogmatism
of the "Raskol" was an effective narcotic. The Russian nobleman
lived the life of a miniature tsar on his estate, and it took centuries
of time, the mighty onrush of Western influence, the persistent
recurrence of agrarian revolts, to lead the best of the noble class to
this question: "What right have we after all to own human beings?"

The life of the Muscovite nobility was appalling in its viciousness,
hypocrisy and lack of ideals. The noble literati of Russia received a
meagre historical heritage, indeed. The nobility of Russia was
wakened into intellectual life as much by the Napoleonic cannon and
the Western ideas as by its own internal process of dissolution. This
presentiment of its own decay fashioned the wisdom and the beauty
of the "manorial" period of Russian literature.

To resume, it was the peculiar condition of life in which the
Russian nobility moved that gave to Russian literature its peculiar
bent, and it appears as an independent factor during a process of

decomposition. It was a plant which flourished on a grave. Lacking the inheritance of inspiring traditions, in its vicious indolence it owed its artistic presentation of heroism and melancholy to the ferment of prescience of death. Before its final passing as a potent factor in Russian literature it takes up an alliance with Slavophilism and the "back to the soil" movement, the last attempt to galvanize its own corpse into a semblance of life. In this late period the Russian literary nobles humbly exclaim: *"Ave Caesar, morituri te salutamus."*

As it was dying of its own viciousness, of new deeds and ideas, its best representatives, Hertzen, Ogareff and Turgeneff, met dissolution half way, hailing death as a deliverer, beyond which they felt a new life opening up for Russia. The literature of the Russian nobility was a testament, a confession, a funeral sermon, but it is pervaded by such earnestness and sincerity and sadness that it will forever remain one of the most beautiful pages in the world's history. It was, moreover, a heroic page, says Andreyevitch, for it had to overcome its history, its habits, the elemental blind love of its own environment, its ancestral gallery, the memories of its childhood.

Slavophilism was an important current in Russian literature. It had its poets, S. Aksakoff, S. Chomiakoff, Ostroffsky; its historians, its publicists, its philosophers. The central idea of Slavophilism was that the future belonged to the Slav. Its dream was a revival of the Byzantine Empire. It was exceedingly complex. Hertzen connects it with the historic and stubborn native opposition to foreign innovations, dating from Peter the Great. The Slavophiles were the heirs of the rebels hanged, quartered, shot down by Peter the Great, of the Dolgorukoff party in the days of Peter II, of Lomonossoff, of Empress Elizabeth, whose ascension was expected to be accompanied by an order to "massacre the foreigners." In a somewhat contradictory fashion the Slavophiles dreamt of tolerance, of liberty, of "Zemsky Sobors," of the abolition of serfdom on one hand and of a return to pre-Peter customs on the other. "Down with St. Petersburg and up with Moscow," was their cry. Rather absurdly they claimed that the West was rotting and the young Russian giant was called upon to battle with the Western culture.

"Russia," writes Aksakoff, "is a quite peculiar land, entirely unlike any European state. . . . All European States are the results of conquest. . . . Their beginning is enmity. The Russian State was the result of a voluntary recognition of authority. The Europeans mistake rebellion and license for liberty."

Equally dissimilar are the religious paths which orthodox Russia and the West with its "Popery" have travelled, and the Slavophile considered the comparison highly flattering to the Russian, ecclesiastically.

Slavophilism went the natural path of a movement which attempts to convince its adherents that they are the sole keepers of all truths. Even Dostoyeffsky's genius failed to save it from a sudden and decrepit senility. Upholders of the patriarchal customs, with a horror of personal freedom and liberty, the Slavophiles went down before the inexorable progress of culture and economic conditions.

We find the next act in the drama of Russian nobility under the sign of Nihilism and Western influence. Gogol's mighty hand angrily forced the Russian nobleman's face into the filth wherein the land-owners lived. His works created an immense impression upon the decaying caste of serf-owners. Turgeneff's wonderful pen pictured those noble parks and old mansions slowly going to wreck and ruin. He truly "wrought while passing through the graveyard of his heart." Turgeneff was above all a poet, an artist, a dreamer. The heroes of his tender brush are men capable only of beautiful impulses, like Rudin, who passes away under the strain of the *Marseillaise*, or given to a still and contemplative melancholy like Lavretsky, like Turgeneff himself. They are "superfluous" men, wearied with a struggle between honor and conscience, easily losing their spiritual balance. Turgeneff himself passionately loves life, but painfully realizes its fleeting, its spectral side. He loves liberty, but realizes man's dependence on forces beyond him. He loves the good and the true, but has no faith in the triumph of that which is good and true.

The dissolution of the nobility's influence was progressing slowly but surely. But side by side with the agricultural there was growing up an urban, a metropolitan Russia. Side by side with the nobleman-idealist there was beginning to raise his head the commoner—realist and socialist as he was. The nobleman *loved* side by side with negation, the commoner *hates* what he denies. A stepson of life, the commoner holds against it all he has suffered. He is a vindictive iconoclast. He fights for his own self. Russian literature henceforth knows the nobleman in the rôle of a penitent. The central figure of Russian literature becomes now the "muzhik," the peasant, and next in importance is the indigent dweller of the city's slums. What Gogol did for the country, Dostoyeffsky did for the city as a novelist and Nekrassoff as a poet, and "the city" in Russia, until some years back, meant St. Petersburg, or perhaps also Moscow.

A remarkable feature of this final stage of the career of the Russian nobility in literature was its passion to reward the "people" for the wrongs and the sins of the upper classes. The "back to the soil" movement, with its fanatical "simplification" of habit, speech and mode of life; the devotion of thousands of refined men and women who buried themselves in the poverty-stricken villages and lived among the peasants, teaching the "muzhik's" children and holding lectures for the benefit of the peasants—these were characteristics of Russian literature in the seventies.

Tolstoy is the connecting link between the literature of the spiritually bankrupted nobility and the later stage of Russian literature. In him was concentrated the penitence of the best of noble literati whose consciousness had been first troubled by the evils of serfdom and by the condition of the rightless mass, the noble writers who had sworn Hannibal's oath against slavery. When he left college he declared in a somewhat pompous speech that he was going to the village to devote his life to the welfare of the seven hundred beings entrusted to him by God. Tolstoy's whole life was a challenge to the Russian noblemen to make good to the people the wrongs of centuries. It was in 1887 that Tolstoy had occasion to investigate the depths of vice in a Moscow lodging house where hundreds of the submerged find shelter. The city, which he had never loved, became to him a nightmare. "Back to the village, to the muzhik," was his cry.

Civilization is founded on the poverty of masses. Individual wealth is legalized robbery, he taught. If the muzhik, whom he idealized, is purer and more moral than we, then we must become more like him, even outwardly. Tolstoy's view of life is that God is not in might but in right; that the foundation of life is the moral consciousness of brotherhood and equality, as dictated by love, and not in any jurid-ical, contractual rights. He preaches the negation of culture as a thing of lies and depravity, and depravity, according to Tolstoy, is living at somebody else's cost. The only knowledge man needs is the knowledge of good and evil. He preached the flight from the growing cities, the return to the soil and the farm. He strove to merge with the people and to fight all official life. He urged the flight to forests and hermitages and mountain nooks, a flight from faith and religion as an obligation, from work as a duty, a flight of the human "ego" from the Church, the State and the market place.

In his determination not to resist evil he is as fanatical as the proud Niconian dissenter who proffered his right cheek when his left was smitten, and went to the scaffold rejoicing in the thought that his slayers perished in putting him to death. He preached non-resistance to evil, but he boycotted the State and taught that war, trade, private ownership and authority were all undisguised evils, and while one might not resist, one should not obey.

In the person of Tolstoy the penitent nobility speaks its last word in Russian literature. The movement towards the people, which taught the nobleman that personal happiness in the face of a wretched peasantry is immoral, and stimulated heroism and love of martyrdom in his heart, simply petered out because of a lack of actual community of ideals and aspirations with the peasantry. The clever men and women who buried themselves in the villages as teachers, peasant doctors, workers, failed to establish a common ground with the "people;" they always remained strangers, "educated" intruders from "above," whose efforts were resented by those whom they were intended to benefit.

Though not a nobleman, the latest Russian writer to acknowledge in despair that in "going below" among the people the educated classes of Russia have suffered moral and intellectual shipwreck, is Leonid Andreyev. Russian literature and Russian intellectual life are now undergoing the depressing realization that in spite of all endeavors, in spite of sacrifices and devotion, the intelligent revolutionaries have failed to establish any point of contact with the miserable and poor. Just as the "back to the soil" movement ended in a crash and a fizzle, the Russian "intelligents" now pass through a period of a distressing moral "Katzenjammer." In his "Darkness," a work published in December, 1907, Andreyev paints a gloomily realistic picture of a revolutionary idealist, who on the eve of the execution of an important terrorist mission for the benefit of the "people" is thrown into surroundings of utter depravity. While at first loathingly repelling the moral lepers, he begins to realize that it is a "disgrace to be good;" that he cannot come among the masses patronizingly, as a "good one," but must become a leper himself. The conclusion is a horrible one, but it is advanced by Andreyev as the answer to the torturing query of the Russian intelligent struggler for liberty: "Why have we not won the people?" and the answer is that they have never been "of" the people.

But now the nobility of Russia has ceased to be a factor in Russian literature. Other movements, other influences are at work moulding and fashioning it into new, but still original form. Literature itself has now ceased to be an art in Russia, and has become a weapon.

38 THE NATIONAL CHARACTER AS REVEALED IN RUSSIAN NOVELS

William Lyon Phelps (1865–1943)

New Haven was the birthplace of William Lyon Phelps and Yale the school at which he taught English literature for more than forty years. A prolific writer and one of the first to promote the study of the contemporary novel and drama, he was also one of the first university professors to introduce the study of Russian writers.

His own studies of Russian fiction led Phelps to postulate certain national character traits. Taking the novels literally, he did not question whether the characters described were true portraits of the Russian people. The Russian writers whom he studied were mostly of upper-class background. Extremely sensitive to impressions, they reflected their own personal reactions to the general Russian environment, and were prone to voice feelings of impotence and frustration, of melancholy gloom, of humility, and of universal love. These were not necessarily responses of the people as a whole. Surely, Phelps's statement that Russia's great need was for "the true gospel" was a reflection of his own cultural background. He was probably thinking of Christianity as practiced in England and the United States, where "every minister knows that it is perfectly safe to preach the Sermon on the Mount every day of the year," given "the healthy moderation of the Anglo-Saxon." Should he not have considered that "your true Russian [who] knows no middle course," whom he found impulsive and tending to excess, might interpret the Sermon on the Mount somewhat more literally?

This selection is from the introduction of his *Essays on Russian Novelists*, published in 1911.[121]

218

THE IMMENSE SIZE of the country produced an element of largeness in Russian character that one feels not only in their novels, but almost invariably in personal contact and conversation with a more or less educated Russian. This is not imaginary or phantastic; it is a definite sensation, and immediately apparent. Bigness in early environment often produces a certain comfortable largeness of mental vision. One has only to compare in this particular a man from Russia with a man from Holland, or still better, a man from Texas with a man from Connecticut. The difference is easy to see, and easier to feel. It is possible that the man from the smaller district may be more subtle, or he may have had better educational advantages; but he is likely to be more narrow. A Texan told me once that it was eighteen miles from his front door to his front gate; now I was born in a city block, with no front gates at all. I had surely missed something.

Russians are moulded on a large scale, and their novels are as wide in interest as the world itself. There is a refreshing breadth of vision in the Russian character, which is often as healthful to a foreigner as the wind that sweeps across the vast prairies. The largeness of character partly accounts for the impression of vastness that their books produce on Occidental eyes. I do not refer at all to the length of the books—for a book may be very long, and yet produce an impression of pettiness, like many English novels. No, it is something that exhales from the pages, whether they may be few or many. As illustrations of this quality of vastness, one has only to recall two Russian novels—one the longest, and the other very nearly the shortest, in the whole range of Slavonic fiction. I refer to *War and Peace*, by Tolstoi, and to *Taras Bulba*, by Gogol. Both of these extraordinary works give us chiefly an impression of Immensity—we feel the boundless steppes, the illimitable wastes of snow, and the long winter night. It is particularly interesting to compare *Taras Bulba* with the trilogy of the Polish genius, Sienkiewicz. The former is tiny in size, the latter a leviathan; but the effect produced is the same. It is what we feel in reading Homer, whose influence, by the way, is as powerful in *Taras Bulba* as it is in *With Fire and Sword*.

The Cosmopolitanism of the Russian character is a striking feature. Indeed, the educated Russian is perhaps the most complete Cosmopolitan in the world. This is partly owing to the uncanny facility with which he acquires foreign languages, and the admirable custom in Russia of giving children in more or less wealthy families, French, German, and English governesses. . . . Russian children think and dream in foreign words, but it is seldom that a Russian shows any pride in his linguistic accomplishments, or that he takes it otherwise than as a matter of course.

Now every one knows that one of the indirect advantages that result from the acquisition of a strange tongue is the immediate gain in the extent of view. It is as though a near-sighted man had suddenly put on glasses. . . .

The combination of the great age of Russia with its recent intellectual birth produces a maturity of character, with a wonderful freshness of consciousness. It is as though a strong, sensible man of forty should suddenly develop a genius in art; his attitude would be quite different from that of a growing boy, no matter how precocious he might be. So, while the Russian character is marked by an extreme sensitiveness to mental impressions, it is without the rawness and immaturity of the American. The typical American has some strong qualities that seem in the typical Russian conspicuously absent; but his very practical energy, his pride and self-satisfaction, stand in the way of his receptive power. Now a conspicuous trait of the Russian is his humility; and his humility enables him to see clearly what is going on where an American would instantly interfere and attempt to change the course of events.* For, however inspiring a full-blooded American may be, the most distinguishing feature of his character is surely not humility. And it is worthwhile to remember that whereas since 1850, at least a dozen great realistic novels have been written in Russian, not a single completely great realistic novel has even been written in the Western Hemisphere.

* It is possible that both the humility and the melancholy of the Russian character are partly caused by the climate, and the vast steppes and forests, which seem to indicate the insignificance of man.—W.L.P.

This extreme sensitiveness to impression is what has led the Russian literary genius into Realism; and it is what has produced the greatest Realists that the history of the novel has seen. The Russian mind is like a sensitive plate; it reproduces faithfully. It has no more partiality, no more prejudice than a camera film; it reflects everything that reaches its surface. A Russian novelist, with a pen in his hand, is the most truthful being on earth.

To an Englishman or an American, perhaps the most striking trait in the Russian character is his lack of practical force—the paralysis of his power of will. The national character among the educated classes is personified in fiction, in a type peculiarly Russian; and that may be best defined by calling it the conventional Hamlet. I say the conventional Hamlet, because I believe Shakespeare's Hamlet is a man of immense resolution and self-control. The Hamlet of the commentators is as unlike Shakespeare's Hamlet as systematic theology is unlike the Sermon on the Mount. The hero of the orthodox Russian novel is a veritable L'Aiglon. This national type must be clearly understood before an American can understand Russian novels at all. . . .

Turgenev first completely realized it in *Rudin*; he afterwards made it equally clear in *Torrents of Spring, Smoke*, and other novels.* *Raskolnikov*, in Dostoevsky's *Crime and Punishment*, is another illustration; he wishes to be a Napoleon, and succeeds only in murdering two old women. Artsybashev, in his terrible novel, *Sanin*, has given an admirable analysis of this great Russian type in the character of Jurii, who finally commits suicide simply because he cannot find a working theory of life. Writers so different as Tolstoi and Gorki have given plenty of good examples. Indeed, Gorki, in *Varenka Olessova*, has put into the mouth of a sensitive girl an excellent sketch of the national representative.

"The Russian hero is always silly and stupid, he is always sick of something; always thinking of something that cannot be understood, and is himself so miserable, so m—i—serable! He will think, think, then talk, then he will go and make a declaration of love, and after that he thinks, and thinks again, till he marries. . . . And when he

---

* Goncharov devoted a whole novel, *Oblomov*, to the elaboration of this particular type.—W.L.P.

is married, he talks all sorts of nonsense to his wife, and then abandons her."

Turgenev's *Bazarov* and Artsybashev's *Sanin* indicate the ardent revolt against the national masculine temperament; like true Slavs, they go clear to the other extreme, and bring resolution to a *reductio ad absurdum*; for your true Russian knows no middle course, being entirely without the healthy moderation of the Anglo-Saxon. . . .

In Russian novels, the irresolution of the men is equalled only by the driving force of the women. The Russian feminine type, as depicted in fiction, is the incarnation of singleness of purpose, and a capacity to bring things to pass, whether for good or for evil. The heroine of *Rudin*, of *Smoke*, of *On the Eve*, the sinister Maria of *Torrents of Spring*, the immortal Lisa of *A House of Gentlefolk*, the girl in Dostoevski's *Poor Folk*; Dunia and Sonia, in *Crime and Punishment*—many others might be called to mind. The good Russian women seem immensely superior to the men in their instant perception and recognition of moral values, which give them a chart and compass in life. Possibly, too, the women are stiffened in will by a natural reaction in finding their husbands and brothers so stuffed with inconclusive theories. . . .

To one who is well acquainted with American university undergraduates, the intellectual maturity of the Russian or Polish student and his eagerness for the discussion of abstract problems in sociology and metaphysics are very impressive. The amount of space given in Russian novels to philosophical introspection and debate is a truthful portrayal of the subtle Russian mind. Russians love to talk; they are strenuous in conversation, and forget their meals and their sleep. I have known some Russians who will sit up all night, engaged in the discussion of a purely abstract topic, totally oblivious to the passage of time. In *A House of Gentlefolk*, at four o'clock in the morning, Mihalevich is still talking about the social duties of Russian landowners, and he roars out, "We are sleeping, and the time is slipping away; we are sleeping!" Lavretsky replies, "Permit me to observe, that we are not sleeping at present, but rather preventing others from sleeping. We are straining our throats like the cocks—listen! there is one crowing for the third time." To which Mihalevich smilingly rejoins, "Good-bye till tomorrow." Then follows, "But the friends talked for more than an hour longer." . . .

It is rather fortunate that the Russian love of theory is often accompanied by the paralysis of will power, otherwise political crimes would be much more common in Russia than they are. The Russian is tremendously impulsive, but not at all practical. Many hold the most extreme views that would shock a typical Anglo-Saxon out of his complacency; but they remain harmless and gentle theorists. Many Russians do not believe in God, or Law, or Civil Government, or Marriage, or any of the fundamental institutions of Society; but their daily life is as regular and conventional as a New Englander's. Others, however, attempt to live up to their theories, not so much for their personal enjoyment, as for the satisfaction that comes from intellectual consistency. In general, it may be said that the Russian is far more of an extremist, far more influenced by theory, than peoples of the West. This is particularly true of the youth of Russia, always hot-headed and impulsive, and who are constantly attempting to put into practice the latest popular theories of life. American undergraduates are the most conservative folk in the world; if any strange theory in morals or politics becomes noised abroad, the American student opposes to it the one time-honored weapon of the conservative from Aristophanes down,—burlesque. Mock processions and absurd travesties of "the latest thing" in politics are a feature of every academic year at an American university. Indeed, an American student leading a radical political mob is simply unthinkable. It is common enough in Russia, where in political disturbances students are very often prominent. If a young Russian gives his intellectual assent to a theory, his first thought is to illustrate it in his life. One of the most terrible results of the publication of Artsybashev's novel *Sanin*—where the hero's theory of life is simply to enjoy it, and where the Christian system of morals is ridiculed —was the organization, in various high schools, among the boys and girls, of societies *zum ungehinderten Geschlechtsgenuss.** They were simply doing what *Sanin* told them they ought to do; and having decided that he was right, they immediately put his theories into

* "For unrestricted sexual enjoyment"—Ed.

practice. Again, when Tolstoi finally made up his mind that the Christian system of ethics was correct, he had no peace until he had attempted to live in every respect in accordance with those doctrines. And he persuaded thousands of Russians to attempt the same thing. Now in England and in America, every minister knows that it is perfectly safe to preach the Sermon on the Mount every day of the year. There is no occasion for alarm. Nobody will do anything rash. . . .

Finally, in reading the works of Tolstoi, Turgenev, Dostoevski, Gorki, Chekhov, Andreev, and others, what is the general impression produced on the mind of a foreigner? It is one of intense gloom. Of all the dark books in fiction, no works sound such depths of suffering and despair as are fathomed by the Russians. . . . Suffering is the heritage of the Russian race; their history is steeped in blood and tears, their present condition seems intolerably painful, and the future is an impenetrable cloud. In the life of the peasants there is of course fun and laughter, as there is in every human life; but at the root there is suffering, not the loud protest of the Anglo-Saxon labourer, whose very loudness is a witness to his vitality—but passive, fatalistic, apathetic misery. Life has often been defined, but never in a more depressing fashion than by the peasant in Gorki's novel, who asks quietly:—

"What does the word Life mean to us? A feast? No. Work? No. A battle? Oh, no!! For us Life is something merely tiresome, dull,—a kind of heavy burden. In carrying it we sigh with weariness and complain of its weight. Do we really love Life? The Love of Life! The very words sound strange to our ears! We love only our dreams of the future—and this love is Platonic, with no hope of fruition."

Suffering is the corner-stone of Russian life, as it is of Russian fiction. That is one reason why the Russians produce here and there such splendid characters, and such mighty books. The Russian capacity for suffering is the real text of the great works of Dostoevsky, and the reason why his name is so beloved in Russia—he understood the hearts of his countrymen. . . .

The immediate result of all this suffering as set forth in the lives and in the books of the great Russians, is Sympathy—pity and sympathy for Humanity. . . . This growth of Love and Sympathy in the Russian national character is to me the sign of greatest promise in their future, both as a nation of men and women, and as a contributor to the world's great works of literary art. If anything can dispel the black clouds in their dreary sky, it will be this wonderful emotional power. The political changes, the Trans-Siberian railway, their industrial and agricultural progress,—all these are as nothing compared with the immense advance that Christian sympathy is now making in the hearts of the Russian people. The books of Dostoevski and Tolstoi point directly to the Gospel, and although Russia is theoretically a Christian nation, no country needs real Christianity more than she. The tyranny of the bureaucracy, the corruption of fashionable society, the sufferings of the humble classes, the hollow formalism of the Church, make Russia particularly ripe for the true Gospel—just as true to-day as when given to the world in Palestine.

39 A COUNTRY OF BIG THINGS

Frederic Austin Ogg (1878–1951)

Another grand, old man in the field of political science, Ogg grew up
on a farm in Indiana. His family moved to the city so that he could
get an education, which led to a long and satisfying academic
teaching career. After holding posts in history at Indiana University,
Harvard, Boston University, and Simmons College, he was appointed
assistant professor of political science at the University of Wisconsin
in 1914. He remained there until his retirement in 1948. A prolific
writer on medieval and American history, the economic and social
development of Europe, and political science, he was also editor of
the *Century Political Science Series* and the *American Political
Science Review*.

In the following article, written in 1915[122] during World War I,
he tried to explain the alliance between the democratic Western
powers and autocratic Russia by describing Russia as essentially
Western-oriented. He believed that Russia's great future in world
affairs would not be affected by an unfavorable outcome of the war.

———————————•

A COUNTRY OF continental proportions, stretching ever monoto-
nously before the traveler's eye, with the sharpest contrast of heat and
cold, of flood and drought, of opulence and misery, of culture and
primitive social conditions; a chaos of races and creeds, and a babel
of tongues; historically in the main, but not wholly, European; a
world within itself and a world between worlds—such is the land
which we know today as Russia.

Twenty-four hundred years ago Herodotus could find nothing

extraordinary about it except the number and size of its rivers. And it is only within days comparatively recent that the civilized world has taken the same interest in the history and life of the great Muscovite dominion which for ages men have felt in the affairs of countries farther west and south.

In point of fact the story of the Russian people, while different enough from that of the French, the Italians, the Germans, or the English, abounds in commanding personalities, extraordinary events, and monumental achievements. In view of the phenomenal rapidity with which the subjects of the Czar—in common with all Slavs— are increasing in numbers, together with the substantial modernization which they are now undergoing, it is as well assured as any great fact can be that in the next fifty years Russia will assume a place of importance in the world well in advance of that which she occupies to-day. No conceivable outcome of the present European war can seriously interfere with the fulfilment of this prediction.

The initial fact to be grasped by one who would understand the Russia of our time is the immensity of the stage upon which the nation's rôle in history has been played. Russia is preeminently the country of big things, and the biggest thing of all is the country itself.

In European Russia alone the State of New York could be set down forty times, with room to spare. In the Russian territory as a whole, covering as it does one-sixth of the globe's land area, and one twenty-third of its entire surface, the Empire State could be set down one hundred and sixty-five times. Russia west of the Urals is ten times the size of France, thirty-three times the size of England and Wales. Among all recorded political creations, not even excepting the Roman Empire, the dominion of the Czar is surpassed in size only by Greater Britain.

There have been nations, and there are some to-day, whose place in history has borne little or no relation to their physical extent. One such was Athens. Others were medieval Venice, the Florence of the Renaissance, and even the England of the pre-colonial era. And among contemporary states, one thinks instantly of Switzerland, Holland, and Belgium.

Russia, however, is far from belonging to this category. With her size has counted for well-nigh everything. Her expansive lands, her enormous distances, her far-flung frontiers—in these it is that one must discover the principal elements of both her historic strength and her weaknesses.

The origins of the present racial composition of the Russian people are problems with which the ethnologists have long wrestled. Just as in France there has been furious debate upon the proportion of the Teutonic, Roman, and Gallic blood in the veins of modern Frenchmen, so in Russia has been discussion, permeated by no small amount of pride, patriotism, and prejudice, of the question whether the Russian of to-day is a mixed or an unmixed Slav, and whether, indeed, he is a Slav at all.

The results have not been at all points conclusive; but it may be said to have been established that the Russians are descended from peoples who were among the later comers into Europe, and also that they are a people of mixed blood, speech, and character. . . .

The predominating element in the modern Russian is, however, . . . Slavic. That the Slavs came originally from Asia there can be no reasonable doubt, although of the time and manner of their westward migration we know nothing at all. . . .

From their earliest appearance the Slavs are described as a kind-hearted, hospitable, liberty-loving, deeply religious people. They lived by agriculture, and they had a social organization which in its essentials has been preserved to this day. The family was controlled by the father. The *mir*, or commune, consisted of a number of families, was governed by a council of the family elders. Several communes combined to form a *volost*, or canton whose affairs also were administered by a council. . . .

The effect of the present war upon the Russian position in the world cannot be foreseen in detail; but it is a safe guess that, whatever happens, the Muscovite empire will be saved by her immensity, her immobility, and her reserve strength from suffering a setback more serious than that from which she so speedily recovered after the war with Japan. Defeat can mean no serious loss of territory or impairment of resources; victory would probably mean accessions, and perhaps very important accessions, to both.

Politically, Russia is one of the great enduring facts of the modern world. Culturally, her rôle has been, and is, likewise of fundamental importance.

As Dante among the great men of history, so Russia among the great nations has been the Janus-faced. Her outlook has ever been in two quite opposite directions. All the troubles and sufferings and miserable discords which run through the life of her people, no less than their achievements and their victories, are the consequence of the intermediate position between East and West which fate has decreed that the nation shall occupy. Europe and Asia still carry on their age-long quarrel within the empire's confine; the imperial emblem, the two-headed eagle, remains a fitting symbol of the nation's dual character. First it was Asia that overflowed Europe; latterly it is Europe which has overflowed Asia.

Russia's rôle in civilization has been to preserve an equilibrium between those forces which are distinctively eastern and those which are distinctively western, and her greatest geniuses have ever reconciled in themselves eastern and western tendencies. As it was with Peter the Great in the sphere of statecraft, so it was with Pushkin in that of poetry, with Solovieff in that of philosophy, and with Tolstoi in that of religion and morals.

But it is important to observe that, at least since the period of Peter the Great, the whole aspiration of Russia in matters of culture has been toward Europe, not Asia. Russia is a Christian nation. Her administrative and economic reforms are planned and executed on Western lines. Her science is the science of France and Germany, and her art, whether sculpture, painting, poetry, or music, is being assimilated ever more completely to European forms and standards of esthetics. No important political, social, or intellectual movement in the West is without its reflection in Russia.

And, even if Russia were several times more Oriental than she is, it would hardly be gracious of peoples situated farther west to taunt her with her un-European character, seeing that through all the centuries she has served them as a protecting buffer against Asiatic invasion and domination.

40 THE ESSENCE OF RUSSIAN PHILOSOPHY AND RELIGION

Leo Wiener (1862–1939)

Born in White Russia and educated in Warsaw and Berlin, Leo Wiener came to America in 1882. He joined the department of Germanic and Romance languages at the University of Missouri in 1892. From 1896 until his retirement in 1930, he was professor of Slavic languages and literature at Harvard, the first position of this kind in the United States. His teaching and his many publications on the subject made him a pioneer of Slavic studies in America, although his interests and activities ranged beyond that field.

According to Wiener, the contradictions inherent in the Russian national life were determined by the country's distance from the focuses of Western culture and civilization. This distance prevented the "elemental forces" of the masses from being deeply affected by the outside world and resulted in a "unique jostling of mythical antiquity and stark reality,—an eternal and inextricable enigma to the Western observer. Hence the totally contradictory valuations which are found in books on Russia, on the basis of the same data."[123] Notwithstanding the existing contradictions or, perhaps, because of them, Wiener believed in the great potentialities and the rich endowments of what he called "the Russian soul." The following selection is from his book *An Interpretation of the Russian People*,[124] published in 1915.

THERE ARE THOSE to whom order and system represent the highest accomplishments of human activities, those to whom obvious efficiency is a criterion of real progress. Men possessed of such minds love to ramble in Italian gardens, with their close cropped and fantastic hedges, and, like Dr. Johnson, abhor green fields and natural forests. These men grade civilization by the sum total of visible results, and recognize the salutary effect of a religion by the splendid churches, gorgeous divine service, organized charity, learned clergy, and refined congregations which they display. To such observers the condition of religion in Russia represents a sad and discouraging spectacle. With the exception of the superb cathedrals of the cities, built by the magnificence of wealthy patrons and supported by all the splendors of modern civilization, the churches of Russia harbor an ignorant clergy and superstitious worshipers, equally devoid of visible organization and cultural tendencies. And the more such observers study the history of the Russian Church, the more they become disappointed and turn away to the more brilliant spectacles represented in the West. Yet it may be shown that Russia has a germ of a far deeper religious consciousness than any other country in Europe, and that a few years of intellectual and political freedom will bring the Greek Catholic Church so prominently to the front, that the older churches of Europe will find it very difficult to compete with it for real efficiency and widespread influence. Even before attempting the analysis of the Russian religion, it is possible to prove this thesis from general considerations.

Russia has shown a uniform weakness in the development of philosophic systems, not because the Russian mind is incapable of assiduous scientific labors, but because it abhors the philosophic void. Abstract philosophy has been the special prerogative of German scholars, who have in this field produced wonders. But their systems, although applicable for scientific theories, have seldom entered into the life of the nation. Hegel, Schelling, Nietzsche have far more affected the daily conduct of Russians, than they have that of the Germans. The study of Russian literature, art, science, political life

is meaningless, if pursued without reference to the German philoso-
phies which have directed the intellectual movements of Russia. The
cause of this is temperamental. The Russian is not interested in the
abstract teleological questions, but constantly wants to find the
logical relation of life's duties to life itself. A French philosopher,
who recently has subjected Russian philosophic ideas to a close
scrutiny, has come to the conclusion that it presents endless new possibilities, because, in contradistinction with Western philosophy, it
strives after a concrete idealism. This characterization is just. As
Vereshchagin objected to the representation of saints on flimsy
clouds, so the philosopher cannot grasp an idealism which does not
immediately give concrete results. He cannot deal with an ideal world.
He is interested in the world in which we live, and only to such a
world does he want to apply his idealism. The Russian philosopher
is a relativist *par excellence*.

If art must be related to life, so must philosophy. As Tolstoy puts
it: "Most striking is the deviation from the fundamental questions
and their distortion in what in our time is called philosophy. It would
seem that there is one question which is subject to the solution of
philosophy, and that is: What must I do? To this question there have
been some kinds of answers in the philosophy of the Christian
nations, though these were connected with the greatest unnecessary
confusion of ideas: such answers were those by Spinoza, by Kant in
his *Critique of Pure Reason*, by Schopenhauer, and especially by
Rousseau. But of late, since the time of Hegel, who recognized
everything in existence as sensible, the question as to what we shall
do has been put in the background, and philosophy directs all its
attention to the investigation of what is, and to the subordination of
this to a previously stated theory." But if philosophy is to give, not
the answer to what life is, but what we shall do with the life which
we have, then ethics and religion are the only branches which can
have any bearing on life, and nobody can be excused for ignoring
them. The artist and the litterateur, the statesman and the priest,
the professor and the layman must be equally interested in the
matter. That such is the case, is amply proved by the whole of
Russian life. Religion, not sectarian dogma and church observances,
but the "concrete idealism" of philosophy is at the basis of everything

good created in Russia, hence philosophy, as a separate branch is ill-represented, while as the background of literary and artistic activity it is ubiquitous.

The failure of this philosophy or religion—call it whichever you like—in the established Orthodox Church is due, as it has been elsewhere, to the fact that religion has been abstracted from the masses and has been entrusted to a selfish, ignorant, brutal, monastic, upper clergy. Fortunately for the masses, this clergy has never systematized its religion into an academic perfect whole, and the people, though ignorant and superstitious, have never been scientifically corrupted into blind worship of authority. A mere spark will enflame them, and religion will return to those for whom it is meant, without having to struggle against centuries of tradition and the insidious perfection of an ecclesiastic system. The signs are already in the air.

RETURN OF THE MIRACLE-WORKING IKÓN

41 RUSSIA WILL BUY, BUY, BUY!

Richard Washburn Child (1881–1935)

Richard Washburn Child, born in Massachusetts into an old colonial family, graduated from Harvard law school in 1906. For the next two years he worked as a Washington correspondent of several magazines. In 1908 he returned to law, and in addition to his law practice he engaged in political and diplomatic activities. He helped to organize the Progressive party in his home state (1911); he worked for the U. S. Treasury (1917–1918); then, after World War I, he conducted for a year studies of reconstruction problems for the British government. From 1921 to 1924 he was ambassador to Italy on the appointment of Harding, whom he had supported. After first working for the election of Herbert Hoover and later for Franklin D. Roosevelt, he gained the position of special advisor to Cordell Hull at the London Economic Conference of 1934.

While ambassador in Rome, Child was greatly impressed by the fascist movement and by Mussolini, whom he admired and whom he assisted in writing his autobiography. Throughout his life Child published articles, short stories, and novels. A popular writer, he flavored his material with dashes of philosophic generalities. This superficiality, as well as the lack of political and economic sophistication, also characterize his articles on Russia, which he wrote as a wartime correspondent. In 1916, when he wrote the book *Potential Russia*, from which this selection originates,[125] that country appeared to him on the level of a colony, dependent on others for consumer goods and economic development. Of course, he was not alone in misjudging the course of Russian postwar development, although some American businessmen, equally mistaken about Rus-

sia's future, contemplated investment opportunities in a less superficial light.

•————————————————————————•

RUSSIA IS our opportunity. A prize is there not only in international
trade but in a worthy international friendship. It will be a piece of
national folly not to see this gain and not to strive for it. But make
no mistake—the opportunity will not come to the door of the stupid,
nor cry at nights beneath the windows of a people without capacity
for international sense. Others will seek for Russian trade, Russian
markets, Russian investment; the chance will not be served up to us
sitting in an easy chair.

We must move. We must be up and at this thing. We must take
those affirmative steps which fortunately are indicated clearly.

We must accept the view that mutual relationship, and particularly
mutual trade relationship, requires, as any mutual benefit arrange-
ment requires, concessions on both sides. . . .

Not to see the opportunity in Russia is to be blind willfully.

The war has awakened Russia.

She has infinite resources and deserves as a nation long credit.

She cannot manufacture all that she needs to-day. Nor to-morrow.

Russia will have to make her own silver-plated forks or she will
have to buy them from England or from us. The demand for silver-
plated forks to supplant wooden spoons must come because so it is
written in destiny, and Russia is a vast, undeveloped field of riches
which from tilled fields and opened mines will produce that resource
by which the civilization of silver-plated forks, vacuum bottles, patent
towel racks, starched shirt fronts, and hideous electric-light fixtures
may be purchased. If Russia does not purchase, she will be the first
of all peoples to reject the terrible boon of progress.

Russia will not reject them. Way down in the center of Russia
searching for a telegraph station, I stopped in a village to spell out a
sign painted on canvas in characters of the Russian alphabet. It
said: "Potash and Perlmutter." It was the movies.

Russia may defeat Germany; it is civilization which will defeat
Russia.

I regret it; perhaps Russia, in spite of all the nonsense that is believed of her cruelties and her barbaric heart, neither of which exists, is sweeter as she is.

But if anyone is to take silver-plated and patented civilization to Russia, it may as well be our own country—the United States. What will it cost? It will cost a tremendous effort that Americans and some official Americans in Russia shake their heads woefully at the idea of an attempt. But the prize is there. It may be a prize in the form of a new market, because if Russia decides to be an agricultural and raw-material country, she will take down the tariff and buy, buy, buy for 170,000,000 human beings. And if Russia decides to try to be a manufacturing country she will put up her tariff and borrow, borrow, borrow. In this case she will want American dollars and American brains.

Either goods, wares, and merchandise, or dollars and efficiency. We have both.

Russia will pay.

She will pay out of her forests, her mines and her fields, out of the hands and brains of her great undeveloped human resource.

Perhaps most of all Russia will pay us by the contact we will gain from a people unspoiled, spontaneous in gladness, without hypocrisy, candid, complacent, whole-hearted. It will be good for us to be viewed from a natural philosophic height which mere education of an individual does not often attain; it will be good for us to learn to know those who see us as children, a bit dirty, romping with material things, with our toys of factories and steel rails and electric signs and chewing gum trusts, until we perspire. It will not hurt us to come in contact with a people who, as a people, suspect that our complicated material civilization is not only a failure, but perhaps an instrument of blight.

Just now we will meet a people reawakened by war and with a new capacity for recognizing the life of the spirit. If a new prophet is to arise with new messages for man it is probable that he will choose Russia rather than any point on the New York Central lines.

Knowing Russia will not only be good for the tired businessman's profit; it will also be good for his soul.

42 THE VICTORY OF THE RUSSIAN PEOPLE

George Kennan

The woefully short interval between the overthrow of the czarist government and new upheavals caused by bolshevist preparations for revolution raised American expectations for a peaceful and democratic renascence of the country. We are concluding this anthology with an excerpt from a March 1917 article by George Kennan,[126] whose life and work we traced before in an earlier selection. Alas, the hopes expressed by Kennan in this article did not find fulfillment.

• ─────────────────────────────── •

THE RUSSIAN REVOLUTION in its relation to the welfare and progress of the world seems likely to be an almost unmixed blessing. Not only will it sow the seeds of democracy in other despotically governed countries, but it will add greatly to the world's material and intellectual resources. Under the despotic regime of the bureaucracy, Russian literature has recently been almost choked to death by the strangling noose of the censorship; but when the novelists, essayists, and poets of the present generation will be set free there will be a new flowering of national culture. The Slavs, moreover, have moral as well as intellectual power; and when their latent capacities are fully developed by freedom and education they will not only make great contributions to science, literature, and the industrial arts, but will exert an uplifting and ennobling influence in the realm that we call spiritual.

238

Notes

1. Thomas Paine, *Common Sense* (Philadelphia, 1776), p. 65.
2. *See* Herodotus, *The Histories*, trans. George Rawlinson (London, 1964), 1:287ff.
3. *See* Lloyd E. Berry and Robert O. Crumney, eds. *Rude & Barbarous Kingdom: Russia in the Accounts of Sixteenth-Century English Voyagers*, (Madison, Wisc., 1968), p. xiii. *See also:* Karl Heinz Ruffmann, *Das Russlandbild im England Shakespeares* (Göttingen, 1952), p. 172; and Fritz Epstein, in *Aufzeichnungen über den Moskauer Staat*, by Heinrich von Staden (Hamburg, 1930), p. 26.
4. Thomas Paine, *Common Sense*, p. 65.
5. Cushing Strout, *The American Image of the Old World* (New York, 1963), p. 1.
6. Philip Rahv, Introduction to *Discovery of Europe* (Boston, 1947), pp. xi–xii. *See also:* Daniel J. Boorstin, *America and the Image of Europe* (New York, 1960), pp. 12, 121.
7. For the origin and development of the earlier version of the "Grand Tour," *see:* William Edward Mead, *The Grand Tour in the Eighteenth Century* (Boston, 1914); Geoffrey Trease, *The Grand Tour* (London, 1967); Lawrence and Sylvia Martin, *Europe: The Grand Tour* (New York, 1967), and in *Saturday Review*, May 27, 1967, pp. 41–43.
8. Peter Parley [pseud. of Samuel Griswold Goodrich], *The Tales of Peter Parley about Europe* (Boston, 1828), pp. v, 135.
9. From his diary, November 28, 1841. *See* George William Curtis, *The Correspondence of John Lothrop Motley* (New York, 1889), 1:113.
10. *New York Herald*, editorial of April 4, 1856.
11. Anna Mary Babey, *Americans in Russia 1776–1917: A Study of American Travelers in Russia* (New York, 1938), p. 124.
12. *See* for example: William Coxe, *Travels into Poland, Russia, Sweden and Denmark* (London, 1784–1790); Donald McKenzie Wallace, *Russia* (London, 1877, 1905); Marquis de Custine, *La Russie en 1839* (Paris, 1843); Anatole Leroy-Beaulieu, *L'Empire des Tsars et les Russes* (Paris, 1881–1889); Freiherr von Haxt-

hausen, *Studien über die Inneren Zustände Russlands* (Hannover, 1847).

13. Philip E. Mosley and John S. Curtis, in *American Research on Russia,* ed. Harold Fisher (Bloomington, 1959), pp. 1, 23.

14. Robert J. Kerner, *Slavic Europe* (Cambridge, Mass., 1918), p. vii.

15. Erik H. Erikson, *Childhood and Society* (New York, 1963), p. 359.

16. *See* especially: Thomas A. Bailey, *America Faces Russia: Russo-American Relations from the Early Times to Our Day* (Ithaca, 1950); Benjamin Platt Thomas, *Russo-American Relations, 1815–1867* (Baltimore, 1930); William Appleman Williams, *American-Russian Relations, 1781–1947* (New York, 1952).

17. Erwin Hölzle, *Russland und Amerika: Aufbruch und Begegnung zweier Weltmächte* (Munich, 1953).

18. Ibid., p. 19.

19. John C. Hildt, *Early Diplomatic Negotiations of the United States with Russia* (Baltimore, 1906), p. 9.

20. Thomas, *Russo-American Relations,* p. 167. *See also:* Walter La-Feber, *The New Empire* (Ithaca, 1963), p. 318; Williams, *American-Russian Relations,* p. 4; Pauline Tompkins, *American-Russian Relations in the Far East* (New York, 1949), p. 5.

21. Williams, *American-Russian Relations,* p. 4.

22. Walter Lacqueur, *Russia and Germany* (Boston, 1965), p. 11.

23. John Howes Gleason, *The Genesis of Russophobia in Great Britain: A Study of the Interaction of Policy and Public Opinion* (Cambridge, Mass., 1967), p. 279.

24. Peter G. Filene, *Americans and the Soviet Experiment 1917–1933* (Cambridge, Mass., 1967), p. 2f.

25. Otto Kirchheimer, "Confining Conditions and Revolutionary Breakthroughs," *American Political Science Review* 59 (1965): 97.

26. This ambivalent attitude is discussed by Russel Blaine Nye, *The Cultural Life of the New Nation 1776–1830* (New York, 1960), and by Bernard Bailyn, *The Ideological Origins of the American Revolution* (Cambridge, Mass., 1967), especially in chap. 2.

27. Racism as an issue and a factor in American politics, domestic and foreign, is by no means an invention or a discovery of present-day radical historians. Its existence and significance has been discussed by Frederick Merk, *Manifest Destiny and Mission in American History: A Reinterpretation* (New York, 1963), pp. 237–247. *See also:* Foster Rhea Dulles, *America's Rise to World Power, 1898–1954* (New York, 1954), pp. 30–32; and Bradford Perkins, *The Great Rapprochement: England and the United States, 1895–1914* (New York, 1968), chap. 4.

28. For a review and bibliography on the question of the existence of

a national character and on theories and studies of its identification, *see* Arvid Broderson, "National Character: An Old Problem Reexamined," *Diogenes* 20 (1957):468–486. *See also: The Annals of the American Academy of Political and Social Science* (Philadelphia) 370 (March, 1967):1ff.

29. Alexis de Tocqueville, *Memoir, Letters and Remains* (London, 1861), 2:251.
30. *New York Magazine* 5 (May, 1792):287–288.
31. Moncure Daniel Conway, *Autobiography: Memoirs and Experiences* (Boston, 1904), pp. 180–181.
32. Raymond T. McNally, "The Origins of Russophobia in France: 1812–1830," *American Slavic and East European Review* 18 (1958):188. *See also:* Michel Cadot, *La Russie dans la Vie Intellectuelle Française (1839–1856)* (Paris, 1967), p. 538.
33. Alexis de Tocqueville, *Democracy in America*, paperback ed. (New York, 1954), 2:176.
34. Bailey, *America Faces Russia*, p. 349.
35. Letter of March 23, 1777. In George Washington, *Writings*, bicentennial ed. (Washington, 1932), 7:317.
36. *Niles' Weekly Register* (Philadelphia) 6 (April 30, 1814):142.
37. Charles Brandon Boynton, *The Russian Empire* (Cincinnati, 1856), pp. 182–183.
38. Orestes Augustus Brownson, *Brownson's Quarterly Review* (New York) 2 (July, 1854):386–387.
39. *The American Catholic Quarterly Review* (Philadelphia) 4 (October, 1879):691–693.
40. For an introduction to this question, *see* Dmitrij Tschižewskij and Dieter Groh, *Europa und Russland* (Darmstadt, 1959), pp. 1–14.
41. John Quincy Adams, "Essay on Russia," Microfilm Reel 238, Miscellany, Item No. 13, Adams papers, Massachusetts Historical Society, Boston.
42. Woodrow Wilson, *The State: Elements of Historical and Practical Politics* (Boston, 1892), p. 620.
43. *See* Elihu Root, *The United States and the War* (Cambridge, Mass., 1918), p. 101.
44. George F. Kennan, *Soviet-American Relations 1917–1920: Russia Leaves the War* (Princeton, 1956), p. 12.
45. Henry Middleton, dispatch of January 30, 1826. In Marc Raeff, "An American View of the Decembrist Revolt," *Journal of Modern History* 25 (1953):290–293.
46. Letter of May 22, 1833. In George Ticknor Curtis, *The Life of James Buchanan* (New York, 1883), 1:187.
47. *Madame de Staël on Politics, Literature and National Character*, ed. Morroe Berger (New York, 1965), p. 340.

48. *Russia's Eastward Expansion*, ed. George Alexander Lensen (Englewood Cliffs, N. J., 1964), p. 37.
49. Letter of September 10, 1783. In John Quincy Adams, *Writings*, ed. Worthington Chauncey Ford (New York, 1913), 5:11.
50. Carl Schurz, *Reminiscences* (New York, 1907), 2:53–56.
51. Letter of January 10, 1904. In Henry Adams, *The Letters*, ed. Worthington Chauncey Ford (Boston, 1930), 2:419–420.
52. Andrew Dickson White, "A Day with Andrew D. White at His Home in Ithaca," *The Craftsman* (Eastwood, N.Y.) 8 (1905):733.
53. Richard Washburn Child, "The Better Half of Russia," *Century Illustrated Monthly Magazine* (New York) 92 (1916):622.
54. Comte de Las Cases, *The Life, Exile and Conversations of the Emperor Napoleon* (London, 1835), 4:87–88.
55. Richard Hofstadter, *The Age of Reform* (New York, 1955), p. 85.
56. Mark Twain, *Tom Sawyer Abroad* (New York, 1896), p. 72.
57. Letter of November 20, 1821. In James Madison, *Letters and Other Writings* (Philadelphia, 1865), 3:235–236.
58. Theodore Roosevelt, *The Letters* (Cambridge, Mass., 1951), 1:646–647.
59. Neill S. Brown, diplomatic dispatch of January 28, 1852. In Joseph O. Baylen, "A Tennessee Politician in Imperial Russia 1850–1853," *Tennessee Historical Quarterly* 14 (1955):250.
60. *See* for example: Boynton, *Russian Empire*, pp. 84–85; Albert Jeremiah Beveridge, *The Russian Advance* (New York, 1903), p. 381; Francis Vinton Greene, "The Genius of Russia," *World's Work* (New York) 7 (1904):4703–4704; Alexander von Schelting, *Russland und Europa im Russischen Geschichtsdenken* (Berne, 1948), pp. 299–313.
61. Russel Blaine Nye, *This Almost Chosen People: Essays in the History of American Ideas* (East Lansing, Mich., 1966), p. 164. *See also* Hans Kohn, "Dostoyevsky and Danilevsky: Nationalist Messianism," in *Reflections on Modern History* (Princeton, 1963), especially pp. 132–134.
62. Schelting, *Russland und Europa*, pp. 308–311; and *The Mind of Modern Russia: Historical and Political Thought of Russia's Great Age*, ed. Hans Kohn (New York, 1962), p. 19.
63. Tocqueville, *Democracy in America*, 1:452.
64. English translation by the editor from the French original in *Sbornik Imperatorskago Russkago Istoricheskago Obshchestva* (St. Petersburg, 1881), 33:293–294.
65. Thomas Paine, *Common Sense*, p. 65.
66. Letter of June 7, 1777. In Silas Deane, *The Deane Papers* (New York, 1887), 2:69.

67. J. Hector St. John de Crèvecœur, *Letters from an American Farmer* (London, 1782), pp. 250–251.

68. Alexander Hill Everett, *America* (Philadelphia, 1827), pp. 13–17.

69. Julius Fröbel, in *San Francisco Journal*, June 16, 1855.

70. Letter of May 7, 1872. In Curtis, *The Correspondence*, 2:336.

71. *New York Herald*, Editorial of April 29, 1867.

72. John Quincy Adams, "Essay on Russia."

73. John Quincy Adams, *Memoirs*, ed. Charles Francis Adams (Philadelphia, 1874), 1:8–9.

74. Instructions to Middleton of July 5, 1820. In James Monroe, *The Writings*, ed. S. M. Hamilton (New York, 1902), 6:348.

75. *John Ledyard's Journey through Russia and Siberia 1787–1788: The Journal and Selected Letters*, ed. Stephen D. Watrous (Madison, Wisc., 1966), pp. 181–182, 202–204, 227–228, 232.

76. *New-York Magazine or Literary Repository* (New York) 5 (May, 1792):287–288.

77. Jedidiah Morse, *The American Universal Geography* (Boston, 1793), 2:56–72.

78. Historicus [pseud.], "Manners and Customs of the Russian Peasants," *Literary Museum or Monthly Magazine* (West-Chester, Penn.), March, 1797.

79. *Literary Magazine and American Register* (Philadelphia) 6 (December, 1806):445–448.

80. Robert Walsh, Jun., *Correspondence Respecting Russia between Robert Godloe Harper, Esq., and Robert Walsh, Jun.* (Philadelphia, 1813), pp. 30–31, 76–77.

81. David Ramsay, *Universal History Americanised* (Philadelphia, 1819), 5:488, 8:93–95, 100.

82. William David Lewis, "Letter to Edward Coles," *Delaware History* (Wilmington, Del.) 9 (October, 1961):330–340.

83. Alexander Hill Everett, *Europe: Or a General Survey of the Present Situation of the Principal Powers* (Boston, 1822), pp. 443–448.

84. Henry Middleton, dispatch of January 30, 1826. In Marc Raeff, "An American View," pp. 290–293.

85. George Bancroft, "Russia," *Literary and Historical Miscellanies* (New York, 1855), pp. 324–333.

86. *United States Magazine and Democratic Review* (Washington) 11 (1842):153–154.

87. G. W. Griffin, *Memoir of Col. Chas. S. Todd* (Philadelphia, 1893), pp. 108–109.

88. John Gerow Gazley, *American Opinion of German Unification, 1848–1871* (New York, 1926), pp. 532–533.

89. Henry Winter Davis, *The War of Ormuzd and Ahriman in the*

Nineteenth Century (Baltimore, 1852), pp. 11–13, 349–350, 361–364, 428.

90. "The Destiny of Russia," *Southern Literary Messenger* (Richmond) 19 (1853) :47–49.
91. *New York Herald*, Editorial of June 17, 1867.
92. *See* selection 22.
93. Eugene Schuyler, "The Russian Peasant," *Hours at Home* (New York) 9 (May, 1869) :17–22.
94. Henry George, Jr., *The Life of Henry George* (New York, 1930), p. 170.
95. Henry George, in *San Francisco Evening Post*, December 7, 1871; and in *State: A Journal of Political Opinion*, April 12, 1879.
96. Edna Dean Proctor, *A Russian Journey* (Boston, 1872), pp. 277–280.
97. Januarius Aloysius MacGahan, *Campaigning on the Oxus and the Fall of Khiva* (New York, 1874), pp. 336–344.
98. *See* Michael T. Florinsky, *Russia: A Short History* (London, 1969), p. 308.
99. Walt Whitman, *The Complete Writings* (New York, 1902), 5: 259–261.
100. *See* Dorothy Brewster, *East-West Passage: A Study in Literary Relationships* (London, 1954), pp. 116–117.
101. Van Wyck Brooks, *The Times of Melville and Whitman* (New York, 1947), pp. 180–181.
102. Cassius Marcellus Clay, *The Life, Writings and Speeches* (Cincinnati, 1886), 1:422–425.
103. Robert G. Ingersoll, *The Works* (New York, 1912), 12:318–319.
104. Edmund Noble, *The Russian Revolt* (Boston, 1885), pp. 180–192.
105. For Kennan's views of Russia, *see also* Francesca Wilson, *Muscovy: Russia through Foreign Eyes, 1553–1900* (London, 1970), pp. 294–306.
106. George Kennan, "A Visit to Count Tolstoi," *Century Magazine* (New York) 34 (1887) :263–264.
107. John William Burgess, *Political Science and Comparative Constitutional Law* (Boston, 1890), 1:31–33.
108. Theodore Roosevelt, *The Letters* (Cambridge, Mass., 1951), 1:646–647.
109. Julian Ralph, "The Czar's People," *Harpers New Monthly Magazine* (New York) 97 (June, 1898) :3–10.
110. Frederick Wells Williams, "The Real Menace of Russian Aggression," *Annals of the American Academy of Political and Social Science* (Philadelphia), vol. 13 supplement (May, 1899), pp. 186–197.
111. Carl Schurz, *Reminiscences*, 2:53–56.

112. Henry Adams, *The Education of Henry Adams* (New York, 1931), pp. 408–414.
113. Letter of August 20, 1899. In *Henry Adams and His Friends. A Collection of His Unpublished Letters*, ed. Harold Dean Cater (Boston, 1947), p. 475.
114. Letter of August 10, 1901. In Henry Adams, *The Letters*, 2:337.
115. Henry Cabot Lodge, "Some Impressions of Russia," *Scribner's Magazine* (New York) 31 (1902) :570–580.
116. Andrew Dickson White, "The Development and Overthrow of the Russian Serf-System," *The Atlantic Monthly* (Boston) 10 (1862) : 551.
117. Andrew Dickson White, *Autobiography* (New York, 1905), 2:98–99.
118. Herbert H. D. Peirce, "Russia," *Atlantic Monthly* (Boston) 90 (1902) :468.
119. Herbert H. D. Peirce, "The Mujik and the New Regime in Russia," *Atlantic Monthly* (Boston) 97 (1906) :106–109.
120. Archibald John Wolfe, "Aspects of Recent Russian Literature," *Sewanee Review* (Sewanee, Tenn.) 16 (April, 1908) :129–136.
121. William Lyon Phelps, *Essays on Russian Novelists* (New York, 1911), pp. 6–34.
122. Austin Ogg, "The Vast Empire of the Czars," *Munsey's Magazine* (New York) 54 (1915) :641–680.
123. Leo Wiener, *An Interpretation of the Russian People* (New York, 1915), pp. 14–15.
124. Ibid., pp. 120–123
125. Richard Washburn Child, *Potential Russia* (New York, 1916), pp. 198–221.
126. George Kennan, "The Victory of the Russian People," *Outlook* (New York) 115 (March, 1917) :547.

Bibliography

Books

Anderson, Matthew Smith. *Britain's Discovery of Russia, 1553–1815.* London, 1958.

Babey, Anna Mary. *Americans in Russia 1776–1917: A Study of the American Travelers in Russia.* New York, 1938.

Bailey, Thomas A. *America Faces Russia: Russo-American Relations from the Early Times to Our Day.* Ithaca, N. Y., 1950.

Berry, Lloyd E., and Crumney, Robert O., eds. *Rude and Barbarous Kingdom: Russia in the Accounts of Sixteenth-Century English Voyagers.* Madison, Wisc., 1968.

Boorstin, Daniel J. *America and the Image of Europe.* New York, 1960.

Brewster, Dorothy. *East-West Passage: A Study in Literary Relationships.* London, 1954.

Cadot, Michel. *La Russie dans la Vie Intellectuelle Française, 1839–1856.* Paris, 1967.

Cross, Anthony. *Russia under Western Eyes, 1517–1825.* New York, 1971.

Dukes, Paul. *The Emergence of the Super-Powers: A Short Comparative History of the U.S.A. and the U.S.S.R.* New York, 1970.

Dulles, Foster Rhea. *Americans Abroad: Two Centuries of European Travel.* Ann Arbor, Mich., 1964.

———. *The Road to Teheran: The Story of Russia and America.* Princeton, 1944.

Fletcher, John Gould. *The Two Frontiers: A Study in Historical Psychology.* New York, 1930.

Gleason, John Howes. *The Genesis of Russophobia in Great Britain: A Study of the Interaction of Policy and Public Opinion.* Cambridge, Mass., 1967.

Groh, Dieter. *Russland und das Selbstverständnis Europas.* Neuwied, 1961.

Haiman, Miecislaus. *The Fall of Poland in Contemporary American Opinion.* Chicago, 1935.

Hildt, John C. *Early Diplomatic Negotiations of the United States with Russia.* Baltimore, 1906.

Hölzle, Erwin. *Russland und Amerika: Aufbruch und Begegnung Zweier Weltmächte.* Munich, 1953.

———. *Geschichte der Zweigeteilten Welt: Amerika und Russland.* Munich, 1961.

———. *Die Revolution der Zweigeteilten Welt: Eine Geschichte der Mächte, 1905–1929.* Munich, 1963.

Jensen, Oliver, ed. *America and Russia.* New York, 1962.

Laserson, Max M. *The American Impact on Russia 1784–1917.* New York, 1950.

Lortholary, Albert. *Le Mirage Russe en France au XVIIIᵉ Siècle.* Paris, 1951.

MacShane, Frank, ed. *The American in Europe: A Collection of Impressions Written by Americans from the Seventeenth Century to the Present.* New York, 1965.

McNeill, William H. *The Rise of the West: A History of the Human Community.* Chicago, 1963.

Mohrenschildt, Dimitri S. von. *Russia in the Intellectual Life of Eighteenth-Century France.* New York, 1936.

Nagengast, William E. *Russia through American Eyes, 1781–1863.* Fort Knox, Ky., n.d.

Nerhood, Harry W. *To Russia and Return: An Annotated Bibliography of Travelers' English-Language Accounts from the Ninth Century to the Present.* Columbus, Ohio, 1968.

Putnam, Peter. *Seven Britons in Imperial Russia.* Princeton, 1952.

Rahv, Philip, ed. *Discovery of Europe: The Story of an American Experience in the Old World.* Boston, 1947.

Ruffmann, Karl Heinz. *Das Russlandbild im England Shakespeares.* Göttingen, 1952.

Sorokin, Pitirim A. *Russia and the United States.* London, 1950.

Stoessinger, John G. *Nations in Darkness: China, Russia, and America.* New York, 1971.

Strout, Cushing. *The American Image of the Old World.* New York, 1963.

Tarsaïdze, Alexandre. *Czars and Presidents: The Story of a Forgotten Friendship.* New York, 1958.

Thomas, Benjamin Platt. *Russo-American Relations, 1815–1867.* Baltimore, 1930.

Tompkins, Pauline. *American-Russian Relations in the Far East.* New York, 1949.

Treadgold, Donald W. *The West in Russia and China: Religious and Secular Thought in Modern Times.* Vol. 1, *Russia 1472–1917.* New York, 1973.

Tschiževskij, Dmitrij, and Groh, Dieter, eds. *Europa und Russland: Texte zum Problem des Westeuropäischen und Russischen Selbstverständnisses.* Darmstadt, 1959.

Wieczerzak, Joseph W. *A Polish Chapter in Civil War America: The Effects of the January Insurrection on American Opinion and Diplomacy.* New York, 1968.

Williams, William Appleman. *American-Russian Relations 1781–1947.* New York, 1952.

Wilson, Francesca. *Muscovy: Russia through Foreign Eyes, 1553–1900.* London, 1970.

Zabriskie, Edward H. *American-Russian Rivalry in the Far East: A Study in Diplomacy and Power Politics, 1895–1914.* Philadelphia, 1946.

Articles

Adamov, E. A. "Russia and the United States at the Time of the Civil War." *Journal of Modern History* 2 (1930) :586–602.

Callahan, James M. "Russo-American Relations during the American Civil War." *West Virginia University Studies in American History,* ser. 1, no. 1 (1908).

Davis, Jerome. "One Hundred and Fifty Years of American-Russian Relations, 1777–1927." *Annals of the American Academy of Political and Social Science* 132 (July, 1927) :18–31.

Golder, Frank A. "The Purchase of Alaska." *American Historical Review* 25 (1920) :411–425.

———. "Russian-American Relations during the Crimean War." *American Historical Review* 31 (1926) :462–476.

———. "The Russian Fleet and the Civil War." *American Historical Review* 20 (1915) :801–814.

———. "The Russian Offer of Mediation in the War of 1812." *Political Science Quarterly* 31 (1916) :380–391.

McNally, Raymond T. "The Origins of Russophobia in France: 1812–1830." *American Slavic and East European Review* 18 (1958) :188ff.

Nagengast, William E. "Moscow, the Stalingrad of 1812: America's

Reaction toward Napoleon's Retreat from Russia." *Russian Review* 8 (1949):302ff.

——. "The Russian Fleet to the United States: Were Americans Deceived?" *Russian Review* 8 (1949):46–55.

Raeff, Marc. "An American View of the Decembrist Revolt." *Journal of Modern History* 25 (1953):286–293.

——. "Russia's Perception of Her Relationship to the West," *Slavic Review* 23 (March, 1964):13–19.

Roberts, Henry L. "Russia and America." In *Russian Foreign Policy: Essays in Historical Perspective*. Edited by Ivo J. Lederer. New Haven, Conn., 1962, pp. 577–93.

——. "Russia and the West. A Comparison and Contrast." *Slavic Review* 23 (March, 1964):1–12.

Szeftel, Marc. "The Historical Limits of the Question of Russia and the West," *Slavic Review* 23 (March, 1964):20–27.

Thorson, Winston B. "American Public Opinion and the Portsmouth Peace Conference." *American Historical Review* 53 (1948):439–464.

Index